W9-BHY-187

LIFE WITH ELVIS

LIFE WITH ELVIS

DAVID STANLEY
with David Wimbish

Fleming H. Revell Company
Old Tappan, New Jersey

Unless otherwise identified all Scripture quotations in this book are from the King James Version of the Bible.

Scripture quotations identified NKJV are from the New King James Version. Copyright © 1979, 1980, 1982 Thomas Nelson, Inc., Publishers.

Color photographs and photo on back cover are copyright © Sean Shaver and are used by permission.

Library of Congress Cataloging-in-Publication Data

Stanley, David, 1955–
  Life with Elvis.

  1. Presley, Elvis, 1935–1977. 2. Stanley, David, 1955–   . 3. Rock musicians—United States—Biography. I. Title.
ML420.P96S62 1986   784.5′4′00924 [B] 86-15631
ISBN 0-8007-1490-3

All rights reserved. No part of this publication may be reproduced, stored in a retrieval system, or transmitted in any form or by any means—electronic, mechanical, photocopy, recording, or any other—except for brief quotations in printed reviews, without the prior permission of the publisher.

Copyright © 1986 by David Stanley
Published by the Fleming H. Revell Company
Old Tappan, New Jersey 07675
Printed in the United States of America

Dedicated to
My Lord and Savior Jesus Christ
(March 25, 1982)

Contents

	Foreword	9
	Acknowledgments	11
	Prologue	13
One	**Your New Big Brother, Elvis Presley**	19
Two	**Fun Times at Graceland**	26
Three	**The Seeds of Rebellion**	44
Four	**At Home With the King of Rock 'n' Roll**	61
Five	**On Tour: 1972–1977**	79
Six	**My Brother the Mystic**	109
Seven	**An Angry Young Man**	118
Eight	**Drugs, Divorce, and an Exposé**	141
Nine	**A Swift Downhill Ride**	161
Ten	**The King Is Gone**	177
Eleven	**The Wasted Years**	193
Twelve	**Yes, Lord**	211

Foreword

What you are about to read is an amazing story. The story of David Stanley and his life as stepbrother to the late Elvis Presley. In plain and simple language David relates what life with the "king of rock and roll" was like. You will get an inside glimpse into the world that surrounded Elvis Presley. It is intriguing and fascinating.

But this is not primarily a book about Elvis Presley. This is a book which declares loudly that God made a difference in the life of a young man. David Stanley has come from the synthetic world of entertainment to the real world of God's grace. This is a book about what God can do in a person's life; it holds the promise that what God has done for David Stanley, He will do for every individual who will allow Him to do so.

David Stanley has a message to tell. His message will touch your heart and challenge you in a very personal way. Once you begin reading, you won't be able to put this book down. You will find great profit to your life by spending time in the pages of this book.

Jimmy Draper, Pastor
First Baptist Church, Euless, Texas
President, Southern Baptist Convention, 1982-84

Acknowledgments

I would like to personally thank the many people without whose help this book would not have been possible:

Our Lord and Savior Jesus Christ, for His unconditional love and for saving my soul; my wife, Kandis, for being the godly mother of my children, and for her love and devotion during the writing of this book; my mother, Dee, for laying the biblical foundations in my life at an early age; my father, Bill Stanley, for giving me life; my big brothers, Billy and Ricky, for their influence and love; my stepfather, Vernon Presley, for being the best father he could be; my father- and mother-in-law, Joe and Gene Lanier, and my brother-in-law, Lindy Lanier, for their love and unceasing prayers; John Dawson, for helping me survive on the road; my pastor, Jimmy Draper, for his guidance and spiritual wisdom; Randy and Elizabeth Draper, for their love and support; the members of the First Baptist Church of Euless, Texas, for their prayers and support; Freddie Gage, for winning the lost at any cost; Bailey Smith, for preaching the message I was saved under; James Robison, for sharing God's love; John McKay, for helping me begin a new life; and my brother, Elvis Aron Presley, for loving me when no one else seemed to and for allowing me to be a part of his life for seventeen years.

Special thanks to:
Dave Wimbish, who was able to put my thoughts into book form; Sean Shaver, for the use of Elvis Presley photos from his personal collection, his help on the final edit, and his personal insight from a fan's perspective; and to the fans, for their undying love for Elvis.

David E. Stanley

Prologue

August 16, 1977

It was a lazy, summer Tuesday, the sort of day when it's hard to get motivated, and nobody wants to work too hard. I got to the mansion shortly before noon, when I was scheduled to go on duty. I thought that if all went well I'd have time to shoot a few games of pool.

Just as I expected, the boss—who also happened to be my stepbrother—was still in bed and had left word that he didn't want to be disturbed before 4:00 P.M. That was pretty much the usual routine. He was rarely out of bed before late afternoon. He always had been a night owl, staying up till all hours, and then sleeping late the next day. But you never knew when he was going to need something; so the staff was on duty twenty-four hours a day, just in case. Just in case he suddenly decided he wanted to fly to Denver or Las Vegas for some reason, or if he just wanted someone to talk to, or needed something.

Life with Elvis Presley kept you on your toes.

But more often than not, nothing unusual happened. So I went downstairs to the poolroom and started shooting pool. Ordinarily, I shot a pretty fair game. But today, there were too many other things on my mind—and I was having a tough time getting anything to fall into the pocket. Elvis had been in one of his rather strange moods the last time I had seen him three days earlier, and I hadn't been able to get it out of my mind.

As I left him, he started to cry and hugged me.

"David, I love you, man!"

"Yeah, I love you, too."

"Well, I just want you to know that I'm not going to see you again. Not here anyway. The next time I see you, it will be on a higher plane."

That sort of talk shook me up. I tried to shrug it off and pretended to make light of it, but it still bothered me. I didn't know why he had been talking like that.

We were supposed to head out on tour tonight, and I wondered how it was going to go this time. The last one had fallen just short of disaster, in my estimation. Elvis's fans didn't seem to notice. He could have stood in front of them reciting nursery rhymes, and most of them would have thought it was a fantastic performance. But there had been times when he just didn't feel like working. Other times he'd forgotten the words to songs he'd been singing for twenty years or more. The new tour was also clouded by the fact that a book was due out any day that was going to show the world the very worst side of Elvis Presley. Elvis knew about the book, which had been written by three former employees, and he was literally worried sick that his fans would turn against him once they read it. To Elvis losing his fans would mean losing everything.

I missed an easy shot and grimaced. Before I could get off another one, little Amber appeared in the doorway. Amber was the eight-year-old niece of Elvis's girl friend, Ginger Alden.

"David ... I think there's something wrong with Elvis!"

"What?"

"I think he's sick!"

"Okay, Amber. I'll be right there!"

Amber ran out of the room, just as Elvis's daughter, Lisa Marie, came running in.

"David, my daddy's sick!"

My first inclination was to pick up the phone, call the hospital, and tell them that Elvis might be coming in. But Lisa yelled at me, "Come on, David! My daddy's sick; you've got to help him!"

About that time, I realized that a siren I had heard in the distance was growing louder and louder. In fact, it seemed to be coming up the Graceland driveway. For the very first time, it occurred to me that something might be seriously wrong with Elvis.

My heart jumped to my throat as I ran up the back stairs, getting to Elvis's bedroom about the same time as Joe Esposito and Al Strada.

Elvis was in the bathroom facedown on the floor, his knees drawn up underneath him. He had a chair in the master bathroom where he liked to sit and read. It was obvious that he had been reading and had tumbled face first out of the chair. A book—something on the Shroud of Turin—lay on the floor beside him.

I walked over and shook him. There was no response.

We grabbed him and rolled him over. I wasn't prepared for what I saw. His tongue was sticking out, and his face was swollen and black.

By this time, my stepfather, Vernon, had come into the room.

"Oh, no!" He began to sob. "My son! My son is dead!"

"No, Dad," I said. "He's not dead! He's gonna be all right!"

But I knew I wasn't telling the truth. Even as the paramedics rushed into the room and began administering first aid, all of us knew the truth: Elvis Aron Presley, the most popular entertainer the world had ever known, the fabled king of rock 'n' roll, was dead at the age of forty-two.

LIFE WITH ELVIS

One

Your New Big Brother, Elvis Presley

The days weren't so bad; but the nights could be awful.

In the daytime there were plenty of things to do: games to play, trees to try to climb, cats and dogs to chase after. But when night came, I felt totally alone, and I cried. I didn't understand. Where was Mom? Where was Dad? Would my brothers and I be here at this boarding school forever?

When you're four years old, you don't understand words like *divorce* and *alcoholic*. All I really understood was that my parents were very far away from me, in a place called Germany. All I knew was that when I needed my mother to hold me, she wasn't there. And even though Dad was a little rough with me, and sometimes acted strangely, I missed him, too.

The year was 1960. The place was Newport News, Virginia. My parents had not been getting along. I knew that. But I still didn't understand why my brothers and I had to stay in this awful place. It wasn't fair! Not that Breezy Point Farm was really such a bad place. It was just that Mom wasn't there.

My brothers, Ricky and Billy, were older than me. Billy was seven and Ricky was six. I doubt if they understood any better than I did what was going on. But they pretended to—mostly for my sake.

Ricky, especially, would try to comfort me.

"David, don't cry!" Then he'd put his arms around me, or affectionately pat my head. "Things are going to get better real soon. You'll see!" He tried hard to be convincing, to sound as mature and sincere as a six-year-old possibly could. Sometimes he sounded like he was on the verge of crying himself—but then, he was "too old" to cry. "David, things are going to get better." He said those words to me more times than I can remember; although I'm sure he was saying them as much for his own benefit as for mine.

Then one morning, Billy woke me up with some terrific news.

"David, David, get up!"

"I'm sleepy." I rolled over, hoping he'd go away.

He didn't. Instead, he yanked the covers away from me. "David, I said get up! I've got some great news!"

I began rubbing the sleep out of my eyes. "What news?" I yawned.

"Mom's coming!"

I sat up, suddenly wide awake. "She is? *Now?*"

"She'll be here this morning. And Mrs. Johnson says we're going to be leaving here. We're going home!"

I couldn't believe it. *Home!* I felt like it was Christmas Eve and I was waiting for Santa Claus to arrive. I was shaking with excitement. I would have set a new world's record for getting dressed that morning, but the buttons wouldn't cooperate. It's hard to get those big buttons into those little buttonholes when your fingers won't stop shaking!

Billy and Ricky and I were decked out in our Sunday best, fitting for such a special occasion. When Mom walked into the lobby that day, I thought she looked like an angel.

I don't remember what she was wearing, or how she had her hair done. But I do remember thinking that I had the prettiest mom in the world.

My mother, Dee, has always been an attractive woman. A petite, five-foot-two-inch blonde, she has always attracted attention. But on this particular day, she could have come walking in with spiked hair and clown makeup on, and I still would have thought she was the most beautiful sight I had ever seen. All three of us boys were talking at once, trying to tell our mother every single thing that had happened to us since we'd last seen her. We scarcely paid any attention to the distinguished-looking man she had with her.

"Boys! Boys," Mom laughed, "you're going too fast!" She bent down and swept us all into her arms at the same time.

Then she stood up and turned to the man beside her. "Billy, Ricky, David, I want you to meet somebody very special. This is your new father, Vernon Presley."

That's all there was to it. All of a sudden, we had a new daddy, and our old daddy was gone—swept out of our lives, just like that. I'm sure it sounds strange. Didn't we cry? Didn't we tell Mom that this man couldn't be our father? The answer is no. Mom told us that Vernon Presley was going to be our new dad, and we just accepted it.

And there was something about Vernon Presley—perhaps it was the twinkle in his eyes—that lowered our defenses. For some reason, we knew he was okay.

"David," he said, smiling down at me, "you and me ... we're going to have a great time together!" He turned to my mother. "This one is a natural-born linebacker!" Then he turned back to us boys.

"Well, I think you boys have been in this place long enough. It's about time we took you home."

Home turned out to be eight hundred miles away in Memphis, Tennessee. It was a long drive, especially for three active boys confined to the backseat of a car. We were all excited, but we didn't seem to be any more excited than Mom was. She kept telling us how things were going to be so good when we got to our new home—and how things were going to be so different from now on.

She also told us that we were going to have a new big brother. His name was Elvis Presley. The way she said it made him sound like somebody really special. But his name didn't mean anything to us at that time. At least, it didn't mean anything to me. But Mom was excited, and that made me excited, too. I couldn't wait to get to Memphis.

The miles seemed to go by so slowly. "Are we there yet?" I must have asked that question every five miles. "Are we almost there?" "How much farther?"

Finally, I got the answer I was waiting for.

"Yes, David. We're almost there. Just about ten more minutes and we'll be home!"

I will never forget how I felt that afternoon as we turned off Highway 51 into the long, circular driveway leading up to the Graceland Mansion.

"Boys, this is it. This is our new house!" Mom was beaming.

Vernon guided the car up to the front steps of the mansion. I had never seen such a huge house in my life. This was more like a castle, or a hotel. My mouth hung open, and my eyes must have been popping out of my head. I pressed my face up against the car window to get a better look.

Ricky, who was sitting in the center, between Billy and me, dug his elbow into my side. "See!" he half shouted, half whispered. "I told you things were going to get better!"

And they certainly had. But I'm sure that even Ricky hadn't expected them to get this much better!

As Vernon and Mom led us into the house, our amazement only increased. It was just as impressive on the inside as it had been when seen through a car window. Beautiful crystal chandeliers hung from the ceiling. To the left was a huge dining room. To the right, an even larger living room. And beyond that, another room, where I could see a gorgeous grand piano. I turned in circles, trying to take it all in. It was so big it was a bit frightening, and I stayed as close to Mom as I could get. This house made the place where Beaver Cleaver lived look like a tiny apartment.

The first person to meet us as we stepped through the door and into the foyer was a vivacious black woman. She was the Presleys' maid, a woman with a wonderful, disarming personality. She made me feel right away that I was somebody important.

"Mr. Presley, it's good to have you home! And this must be Dee! She's absolutely beautiful. Welcome to Graceland, Mrs. Presley!

"And these are your boys? I am so glad you boys are here! It's going to be fun having some children around here. I think that's what this place has been missing." Her smile said that she meant it. She really was glad to meet us. She really was happy that we were moving in. I liked her immediately. And even though Graceland's size was still frightening, it was already starting to seem like home.

Our new father led us down the hall and then down some stairs to the basement. There were several more rooms downstairs, and we went into one of them and waited while the car was being unloaded. I sat on the sofa next to my mother, while Billy and Ricky looked around the room. There were a lot of gold records on the walls. A movie projector sat on a shelf in the corner, while a movie screen stood against one wall.

In a few minutes, Vernon came back into the room. He had someone with him—a tall, thin young man with the bushiest sideburns I had ever seen. Beyond the sideburns, I remember his piercing blue eyes and his friendly smile.

I remember, too, that Mom seemed especially nervous when he came into the room.

"Boys," Vernon announced, "this is your new brother! This is my other son, Elvis."

Elvis Presley was twenty-five years old, and I suppose he was not exactly what I expected. He didn't look like the sort of brother who was going to enjoy crawling around in the dirt, playing cars with me. I wasn't disappointed; I was just a little surprised.

"So these are my new brothers!" Elvis exclaimed. He

walked over and picked us up, one at a time, and hugged us.

"I've always wanted a little brother," he said, "and now I have three of them! This is wonderful!"

There was something about Elvis Presley that made me feel loved. Something about his voice and about the strength in his hands when he picked me up and hugged me. Many of the people who knew Elvis will tell you that—there was just something about him!

I didn't know that he was the most popular entertainer in the world, or that he had already sold millions upon millions of records. All I knew was that he was my new big brother. And even though I had just met him for the very first time, I really believed that he was delighted to have me as his brother. I'm sure it sounds funny, but I *knew* right there and then that I loved him and that he loved me. When Elvis picked me up and hugged me, it was as if all those lonely times in that boarding school in Virginia just melted away. All those lonely nights when I had cried myself to sleep suddenly seemed unreal. For the first time in two long years, I felt that somebody really and truly loved me.

He put me back down. "I'm sorry, boys, but I have to get going." He looked at his watch. "I'm leaving right away for Los Angeles. I'm doing a movie out there.

"But when I get back, we're going to have a great time. I promise you!"

He gave each of us another hug, and then he left.

We spent the rest of that day moving into our half of the Graceland Mansion. Or at least the grown-ups did, while my brothers and I, feeling a bit adventurous, went exploring.

Graceland sits on fourteen acres of gently rolling land within the city of Memphis. Highway 51, a busy road dotted with churches, car dealerships, fast-food restaurants, and other businesses, runs right in front of the mansion. To the back and sides of Graceland are typical middle-class neighborhoods. In other words, Graceland is not a secluded estate, surrounded by other secluded estates. It's more like a park, sitting in the middle of Tennessee's largest city.

As we looked around that day, we discovered dozens of the best climbing trees you've ever seen. There were plenty of open spaces, too! Places that would be just perfect for baseball, or football, or for just running and acting silly. The more we saw, the more we liked, and the more it seemed that all of our dreams had come true.

I fell into bed that night, exhausted from all of the excitement of the day. I had a feeling of peace and happiness, and when my mother reminded me to say my prayers, I thanked the Lord for being so good to me.

The next morning, the good dream got even better. When we got dressed and went outside, my brothers and I discovered that Christmas had come early in 1960. Not only had it come early, but it was the biggest Christmas we had ever known. There on the patio were three bikes, three wagons, three footballs, three stuffed animals, three of just about every toy we could have wanted. All of these things came with love from our new brother, Elvis. Even though he was rushing off to the West Coast to finish filming a movie, he still took the time and effort to welcome us into his family in that way.

That's the kind of brother Elvis Presley was.

As we played with our new toys that morning, I'm sure we all must have been thinking the same thing. The song was right: Fairy tales *could* come true! Or at least, that's the way it seemed.

Two

Fun Times at Graceland

I quickly became accustomed to life at Graceland.

When Elvis was gone, life in my new home was slow, moving along at an unhurried pace. Ricky and Billy were in school, and I would be going to school soon. But in the meantime, I was having a ball exploring the property, getting to know the best places for all the games I liked to play.

Most important, Mom was there. And I was already beginning to think my new father was a pretty good guy. At first, for a short time, I missed my real father. But because he was in the military, he had been gone much of the time anyway. So after a while, I just didn't think about it anymore.

When Elvis came home, things really changed. When he was around there was an excitement that hung in the air like static electricity. You could almost feel the mansion pulsating with excitement.

Of course, when Elvis came home, a lot of other people came too. When he was there, so were most of the regulars—the men who accompanied him when he was on the road, whether he was on a movie location, on a concert tour, or spending a few weeks relaxing on the ski slopes. Their being there added to the feeling of hustle and bustle.

But the truth is that Elvis's mere presence always brought a dimension of excitement. In fact, in later years, I could almost always tell when Elvis was home. I would drive up in front of the mansion with a friend who would ask, "Is Elvis here?" I would sit and just sort of listen for a minute, and then I would say, "Yeah, he's here," or, "No, he's not here right now." I can't remember ever being wrong. I don't know what it was, and I certainly wouldn't try to explain it—but he had an amazing presence. I think that helps to account for his fantastic popularity.

I remember, too, that one of the things I learned quickly about Elvis Presley was that he had quite a sense of humor. He would sit at the dinner table and tell funny story after funny story about things that had happened during the latest filming. He would have everyone laughing, including me, even though I was so young that I sometimes didn't understand the stories at all. But they made everyone laugh, and so I laughed right along with them.

I still didn't understand that my new big brother was a famous entertainer. But I was learning that he was a good guy, and I loved being around him. It was obvious that the world of Graceland revolved around him, and it began to seem as though the rest of the world did, too.

I suppose all the talk of movies and songs just didn't sink in. It wasn't unusual for Elvis to sit down at the piano in the music room and play and sing a few songs. I always enjoyed that, but I didn't really appreciate the fact that I was listening to a free concert by the king! (I remember going to my first "real" Elvis Presley concert at Memphis's Ellis Auditorium in 1961. When Elvis came out on stage, all the people started yelling and screaming. I started to cry because I thought something was wrong. It wasn't until later that I came to understand that the screaming was caused by excitement over Elvis's performance.)

Elvis had promised that when he got home from Los Angeles, we were going to have a great time, and he kept his word. As soon as he got back, the fun started. There were movies just about every night, fireworks, and every once in a while Elvis would rent out the Libertyland Amusement Park or the fairgrounds. He would take us, along with the children of his employees, and we would have the park all to ourselves. Sometimes, when we boys were finding it hard to stay awake, Elvis would give us each half of a Dexedrine. He told us they were "stay-awake pills." And that they were. I wouldn't sleep for three days after taking a half of one of those things!

But it was all very innocent. Elvis had no intention of giving us anything that would be harmful. It was just that he was used to sleeping during the day and then being up most of the night. Of course, Elvis didn't have to get up and go to school in the morning!

Looking back on it now, I don't know how we did it. It wasn't that we were out late every night. But we came pretty close, at least when Elvis was home.

When I started school, I found out that being Elvis's brother was not always a picnic. It was terrific in a lot of ways, but it caused its share of problems, too. For one thing, a lot of the kids seemed to resent it when my brothers and I were dropped off at school every day in a pink Cadillac. Even some of the teachers seemed to resent the fact that I was Elvis Presley's brother.

I was often told that I should expect to be treated like any other student—and that if I thought I was better than anybody else, I was wrong. I was teased a lot, and people would tell me that nobody liked me and that the only reason anybody was nice to me was because they wanted to get close to Elvis. That sort of teasing left scars that took years to heal. Then there were those who thought they would get their kicks from beating up on Elvis Presley's little brother. When I was in the third grade at Graceland Elementary School, five older kids ganged up on me in the school rest room.

"Hey! Look, it's Elvis Presley's stupid little brother!"

I tried to leave, but one of them grabbed me.

"Where you going, punk?"

"I was just. . . ."

"You think you're tough, just because your brother's famous, huh?"

They started pushing me around, telling me they were going to knock my teeth out. The only thing that prevented them from trying was that a teacher came in and stopped it. I wasn't really hurt, but I was scared. It got to the point where I hated to go to school, because of all the teasing and abuse I took. The only positive thing about all of this was that I learned to defend myself at a very early age.

But if school was a hardship, the rest of life was pure fun. And I think Elvis enjoyed it every bit as much as we did! Elvis was twenty years older than me, but in a lot of ways I still feel as though we grew up together.

Elvis clowned around with us, we acted silly together, and competed against one another in a variety of contests, mostly having to do with speed. Elvis's life was a whirlwind in those years. He was making movies, recording albums, and taking care of other business. Looking back on it now, I don't really know how he found so much time to spend with us. But he did, and it just seemed natural then.

First of all, there were the go-karts. Everybody had to have a go-kart. We started off with the regular little go-karts with lawnmower engines. It didn't take long for Elvis to get bored with them, though, and we upgraded to the more sophisticated chain-saw-engine go-karts that topped off at around seventy miles per hour.

We spent hours racing around the driveways of Graceland at close to top speed. And that's a pretty small track to be going around that fast! Some of Elvis's friends and employees, like Joe Esposito and Charlie Hodge, would join us sometimes. But more often than not, it was Elvis and us boys.

On one occasion, we were involved in a heated race, and Ricky got a bit too reckless. He was taking a corner at close to top speed, and he cut it a little too sharply. He bounced off a curb and his kart went flying up in the air. It was like watching something in slow motion as his go-kart did three complete somersaults! Elvis always made sure that we wore protective clothing, so, thankfully, Rick was not hurt—he walked away from the accident.

Elvis thought it was about the funniest thing he had ever seen. He and Joe Esposito laughed until they couldn't laugh anymore. Elvis quickly gave Rick the nickname Reckless Rick. The name stuck for quite a while, and there were several more times when it seemed very appropriate.

But that was the closest anyone ever came to being severely injured in one of our races.

*   *   *

In 1962, we moved into a house on Hermitage Street, several miles from Graceland. We lived there while another house was being built for us on Dolan Street, which is just in back of Graceland. Even while we lived in the house on Hermitage, we spent a great deal of our time with Elvis at Graceland. And when we moved into the house on Dolan, all we had to do was walk through a couple of gates and we were on Graceland property.

Also in 1962, a beautiful girl came to live with us in our house on Hermitage. Her name was Priscilla Beaulieu, and she was Elvis's love from Germany. Priscilla was not yet through high school, but Elvis had talked her parents into letting her come from Germany, where her father was a captain in the U.S. Air Force, to live with us in Memphis. He had promised her parents that he would see to it that she finished high school. Then, he would marry her.

That Elvis, an internationally famous entertainer, could talk a teenage girl's parents into such an arrangement is just another indication of how charming he could be. At the same time, Elvis really did love Priscilla, and I know he was able to make her parents understand that. There isn't much that can stand in the way of true love!

I'm sure that being so far away from home and moving in with a family she didn't really know was hard for Priscilla. But she seemed to adjust very well, and I, too, loved her almost from the very beginning.

Priscilla was beautiful, even at that age. She had the biggest, clearest blue eyes I had ever seen and an absolutely flawless complexion. It was no wonder that Elvis had fallen for her. I thought she was just about perfect and had quite a crush on her myself. Elvis would tease me good-naturedly every so often about trying to steal his girl friend. Priscilla and I did spend quite a bit of time together, probably because I was the youngest of the boys and accepted her so totally and so quickly. In addition to being beautiful, Priscilla was also loads of fun.

Sometimes she would put heavy mascara around her eyes and pretend that she was a vampire.

"David, I vant to bite you!" she would say in her best Bela Lugosi accent. Then she would chase me around the house as I pretended to be terrified.

"I'm going to drink all of your blood!"

I would scream and shut myself in the closet. But Priscilla would always catch me and pretend to bite my neck, while I laughed hysterically.

Then it would be my turn to be the vampire, and I'd chase Priscilla around the house.

On my seventh birthday she took me out and spent the whole day with me. It was one of the best birthdays I ever had. First, we visited a toy store.

"Just pick out what you want, David, and I'll get it for you."

I couldn't choose between a neat toy helicopter and a skateboard. I'd put up the skateboard and get the helicopter. Then when we would be heading for the checkout stand, I'd change my mind. I'd put back the helicopter and grab the skateboard. I just couldn't decide, and the indecision was killing me! Priscilla finally resolved the situation by buying both of them.

From the toy store, we headed to the pet shop. We left there with a parakeet and a goldfish. Then she bought me lunch. I had an absolutely perfect time! The best thing about it, though, was all the attention she gave me.

* * *

Another one of my favorite people was Colonel Tom Parker, Elvis's manager. In recent years some bad things have been said and written about Colonel Parker. It is true that the colonel made a fortune off of Elvis's success, but Elvis always figured that he deserved it. He knew that Colonel Parker was a shrewd businessman and he trusted his judgment. The colonel was a tireless worker, and he certainly deserves some of the credit for Elvis's amazing popularity. He found a marketable commodity, he developed it, and he was rewarded very well.

I have also read that Colonel Parker was extremely tight with a dollar. That may be true, but you couldn't prove it by me! He spoiled us rotten with stuffed animals, toys, and other presents.

He also presented me with my first cigar. Come to think of it, I guess he also gave me my last cigar. But that was easy, because my first cigar *was* my last cigar.

I was eight years old at the time and visiting with the colonel in the living room at Graceland. He was waiting for Elvis to come down from his room. The colonel was getting ready to light up a cigar, and he must have noticed that I was watching him.

He pulled another cigar out of his pocket and held it out to me as if it were no big deal.

"Where are my manners? David, would you care for a cigar?"

I didn't know he was teasing.

"Sure!"

I took the cigar and put it in my shirt pocket. I looked around to make sure nobody saw me take it.

"Uh . . . excuse me . . . but I just remembered . . . I forgot to do something."

"Okay, David, you go right ahead."

Within five minutes, I was back in my bedroom with my brothers.

"What is it?" Billy asked, after Rick and I had signaled him to join us.

"Shhhhh!" I gave him a dirty look.

"David's got a cigar!" Rick whispered.

We passed it around, each smelling it and looking at it as if it were some sort of gift from the gods.

"You're not gonna light it, are you?" Billy asked.

"Why not?"

"Because we'll get caught."

"Who's gonna find out?"

Rick lit the cigar and took a puff. He offered it to Billy, who declined. He then passed it to me. I didn't know what to do, and I blew into it.

"No, stupid!" Rick shook his head. "You're supposed to suck on it!"

When I did, I began choking and coughing.

Almost immediately, Vernon was knocking on the door.

"What are you boys doing in there?"

"Uh . . . nothing, Dad." Billy tried to sound as calm as possible.

What were we going to do?

"Let me in! Right this minute!"

"Okay, Dad." In a moment of sheer panic, I stuck the burning cigar in my pants pocket, while Rick went to unlock the door and let Dad in.

Vernon strode into the room, which was thick with cigar smoke. He looked at me. "David! Your pants are on fire!"

I screamed, grabbed the cigar out of my pocket, and threw it under the bed. Vernon grabbed me and began hitting at my smoldering pocket with his hand. "Billy, get under there and get that cigar!"

Of course, we all started blaming one another, and then Colonel Parker. Dad looked awfully angry. Not only had we been smoking, but I had also ruined a good pair of pants, and we had come close to setting the house on fire.

I was sure I was going to get the spanking of my life. But then, all of a sudden, Vernon started laughing. He couldn't seem to help himself. And we knew that we had been spared.

*　　*　　*

When Elvis was home, it was time for the fun to really get going.

One morning, when we still were living in our house on Hermitage, we woke up to find that Memphis had been hit by a huge snowstorm. With sixteen inches of snow on the ground, school was canceled until further notice. It was every boy's wish come true!

My brothers and I were just sitting down to breakfast, when a white limousine pulled up in front of the house. Elvis and his driver got out and quickly shoveled a path to our front door.

Elvis was bundled up like a Eskimo.

"Get the boys ready, Dee. I want them to come with me."

"But I don't know if—"

"Oh, come on, Dee! I'll take good care of them. We can't let this good snow go to waste . . . can we guys?" He gave her that boyish grin.

"Well. . . ." She still wasn't convinced.

"Come on, Mom! *Please?*" we begged.

"Oh, . . . all right. If I say no, I'm sure I'll never hear the end of it!"

That was the way it usually went. Mom would fuss about it and say she wasn't sure if she was doing the right thing—

but she would just about always give in to Elvis.

So we spent the next three days at Graceland with him. We had snowball fights, rode discs down the driveway and snowmobiles across the property. Anytime that Elvis was having fun like that, he wanted to share it with his brothers.

He especially loved anything to do with speed, and that made snowmobiles a favorite pastime. I got the same kind of thrill out of moving as fast as possible, so it was usually Elvis and me looking for the steepest hill or the fastest track. With the snowmobiles in particular, we would look for hills and bumps to help us get airborne.

When there wasn't snow on the ground, Elvis would take the skis off the snowmobiles and put wheels on them. Those things can really move, even when there isn't any snow!

Then there were the golf carts. We had hours of fun racing around Graceland in golf carts. I was undisputed king of the golf cart, since I was the only one who could zip around Graceland on two wheels.

But if we weren't roaring around the Graceland property at speeds in excess of sixty-five miles per hour, then we might be involved in something even more dangerous.

Like fireworks. Elvis loved fireworks. Every Fourth of July, every New Year's Eve . . . and other "special" occasions in between, Elvis would go out and buy four or five thousand dollars worth of fireworks—buzz bombs, Roman candles, skyrockets, and other types of aerial displays. We would split up into teams and turn Graceland into a battlefield!

We'd put on flight suits, gloves, racing helmets, goggles, and rags across our faces. Then we'd get involved in a full-scale war, with five or six "soldiers" on each team. We would take huge fireworks, meant for aerial displays, and shoot them at one another. We would hit tables and turn them over—and if you ever got hit by one of those things, you *knew* it. It's a wonder that we didn't have any serious injuries, but we never did.

Elvis would get a twelve-pack of Roman candles and

touch the whole thing off at once. He would become absolutely maniacal, running around, yelling like a kamikaze, shooting fireworks at anyone in sight!

The closest we ever came to a serious injury was one Fourth of July when I was on Elvis's team.

"David, look out!"

Elvis yelled a warning to me and then shot into the tree, where Rick was getting ready to blast me.

I saw one of Elvis's employees, Richard Davis, trying to sneak around the side of the house.

I let a buzz bomb fly in his direction.

Ka-blam! The thing blew up right in his face. For a moment, I thought I had killed him.

When I got to him, I discovered that the goggles he had been wearing were melted all around his eyes. His face was red and sore around one eye, but other than that he was all right. A truce was put into effect until Richard left to get his eye treated. But as soon as he was safely off the property, the battle started up again.

Our fireworks battles started several fires on the Graceland property—and a couple of times the house itself caught fire. Thankfully, there was never any severe damage.

The closest we ever came to burning the entire place down was when a fireball landed in the area where all the fireworks were kept.

There was a long, green carport at Graceland. And in one section of that carport, Elvis had several boxes full of fireworks—over five thousand dollars worth. One night, our battle came a little too close to the carport.

The next thing we knew, it looked like the whole place was going up in one last blaze of glory. Fireworks were shooting up out of the boxes and hitting the carport's roof; then they would ricochet off and start coming out the sides. You would have thought World War III had started.

For twenty minutes the explosions continued, while we all hugged the ground, afraid to move. All you could hear were explosions, whistles, and what sounded like heavy artillery smashing into Ferraris, Cadillacs, and other expensive cars. The fire department was trying to get onto the property, but they couldn't do anything until the explosions stopped.

In the middle of all this, Elvis was rolling on the ground, laughing hysterically.

Finally, everything stopped. We waited a minute to make sure the coast was clear. Then we scrambled to our feet and began dusting ourselves off. Elvis looked around, surveying the damage.

"Well, that sure was fun," he said. "But it looks like it's gonna cost me a lot of money!" He was right. It did.

Another thing Elvis liked to do with fireworks was to take a chaser and throw it into his grandmother's room. A chaser is a firework that makes a very loud whistling noise, and it flies around in a crazy pattern, like a balloon with the air gushing out of it.

"Grandmother! Got something for you!"

Elvis would open her door and throw one of those things in her room.

"Elvis!"

She would come running out into the hall, while Elvis ran from her, laughing. It's a wonder he didn't give the elderly woman a heart attack, but she always took it with the attitude that "boys will be boys." And for Elvis, it was just another way of telling her he loved her. A rather strange way, true, . . . but that was Elvis!

Another, much tamer passion of Elvis's began when Priscilla bought him a slot-car racing track. This was during the time when you could find public slot-car tracks in just about every city across America.

As soon as Elvis got slot-car fever, all of the rest of us caught it, too. That's the way it always was. Elvis would get caught up in something, and all of the rest of us had to get caught up in it with him, whether we wanted to or not. Pretty soon, Elvis got bored with the slot-car track Priscilla had given him, so he had another one built. Elvis's new slot-car track was so big, he had an extra room built on the Graceland property just to house it.

We spent many hours in that room—the blue room—sometimes all night, racing against one another. Naturally, Elvis always had the fastest car, and so he usually defeated all challengers.

But, as with many of his interests, Elvis overdid it with the slot-car track. When he was interested in slot-car racing, he was almost obsessed by it. If you needed him for some reason and didn't know where he was, the first place to look would be in the blue room. Chances are, he'd be there dueling with some of his employees—Sonny or Red West, Joe Esposito, Charlie Hodge, Lamar Fike—or going one-on-one against me, Rick, or Billy. But within a couple of months, he had completely lost interest. He dismantled the track and gave the whole thing to a Boys' Club. He moved all of his gold records and other awards into the blue room, which became his trophy room.

There were a few passions that remained constant, however, and one of them was horses. Elvis had always loved horses, although most of his life he had admired them from a safe distance. But when he decided to take up riding, he discovered that he loved it. And, as I said before, whatever Elvis liked to do, the rest of us learned to like, too. If Elvis loved to ride, the rest of us loved to ride. Life at Graceland was family togetherness at its best.

He had several horses at Graceland. There was Sun, his palomino; Bear, his Tennessee walking horse; Domino, who belonged to Priscilla; and other horses for the rest of us to ride.

There were always people hanging around the Music Gate at Graceland, hoping to get a glimpse of Elvis. Every now and then, he would ride down to the gate on horseback and spend an hour or so signing autographs and talking to people.

Eventually, Elvis's love for horses prompted him to buy a ranch in Mississippi, just south of Memphis. He named it the Circle G Ranch, and we all spent a lot of time riding horses there. We'd dress up in our cowboy outfits and have a great time. Some of us may not have been able to ride very well, but we sure dressed the part.

One time, Rick decided that he was going to show off a little bit, even though he wasn't the world's best rider. I don't remember exactly what he did, but whatever it was, the horse he was riding didn't like it one bit. That horse took off like a shot—with Rick hanging on for his life.

All I saw as that horse whizzed past me were Rick's blue eyes, looking about three times larger than normal . . . and his thick blond hair, blowing in the wind. We all took off after him, with Elvis in the lead.

Since the Circle G covered 650 acres, it looked as though Rick might be in for a long ride. But Elvis managed to save the day. He maneuvered his horse alongside Rick's. For several seconds, they matched each other, stride for stride. Then Elvis reached out and grabbed Rick, pulling him off his runaway horse and onto Sun.

The whole thing was like a scene from one of Elvis's movies. And we couldn't help but give him a big round of applause when he came riding back to us, with Rick sitting in front of him.

*   *   *

Another constant passion for Elvis Presley was his interest in guns. He loved to shoot, and we would sometimes have target practice in the backyard. And I'm not talking about .22-caliber rifles or even 10-gauge shotguns. We'd shoot .357 magnums, Thompson submachine guns, M-16s . . . just about everything except bazookas! Even today, there are still bullet holes in some of the Graceland buildings, where someone got a little trigger-happy!

Elvis was fascinated with guns, and he built up quite a collection. He was also an excellent marksman.

When I was eleven, several of us went hunting snakes in Mississippi. Someone had discovered a lake out in the country that was literally crawling with poisonous snakes. So we all put on heavy rubber boots, armed ourselves to the teeth, and went down there to clean the snakes out. Even with the boots on, you had to be especially careful to watch where you were stepping. Sure enough, Elvis's cousin Billy Smith stepped right on the tail end of a mean-looking snake. He didn't even see it, but that snake was rising up right between Billy's legs.

Elvis quickly aimed his shotgun.

I yelled, "Elvis, you can't!"

KA-BLOOM! His answer was a loud blast from his gun, which blew the snake's head off and just about sent Billy into cardiac arrest.

Elvis turned to me with that famous sneer on his face. "I can't do what?" he asked.

That same year, when I was in fifth grade at Graceland Elementary School, Elvis began to take a keen interest in my football career. Football was one of his abiding loves, and he was delighted that I had taken up the sport. By this time, I was one of the biggest and most aggressive boys in my class, and Elvis and Dad figured I had the potential to be a good football player.

The first time Elvis came out to one of my practices, all of the kids were trying to get a look at him, and so were the coaches. The practice was a total washout. The next practice was better attended than most of our games. The bleachers were full of parents. It would be nice to say they came out to watch their boys practice, but the truth is that word had gotten around that Elvis might be there. He came twice a week for several weeks, and our practices continued to be very well attended.

While I was happy that Elvis was interested, I often wished he would go a little easier on me. He was harder on me than my coaches were. "Come on, David," he would yell, cupping his hands around his mouth, "you missed your man!" When there was a break, he would call me over to the sidelines. "Man, you've got to hit that guy *harder*. You've got to knock him on his can!" Eventually, I dislocated my knee, and my football season was over. Elvis came to the hospital to see me and gave me a football. A photograph of him presenting me with the football wound up in the *Memphis Commercial-Appeal*.

I'm sure my injury disappointed Elvis, but he didn't let on. It was just that he loved football so much. During the football season, it wasn't uncommon for Elvis to have several television sets tuned in to different games at the same time. He had three sets side by side in one room, just so he could watch all the bowl games on New Year's Day.

There were many touch football games on the Graceland grounds in those days, and they could be pretty rough. Elvis always did his best to win, and he expected everybody else to play that way, too. There were no breaks for anyone. I was expected to play as hard as everybody else, even if I *was* only a boy.

(I ought to add that Elvis was a pretty good quarterback. He had a nice, soft touch as a passer. But he wasn't too happy when one of his passes was picked off!)

*　　*　　*

In 1967, Elvis did something that really surprised me. He married Priscilla. Priscilla had been around for so long that I was beginning to think they would never get married. By now, I was totally familiar with Elvis's image as a swinging bachelor, and I assumed he would keep it that way forever.

Mom and Dad had flown off to Las Vegas a couple of days before, so I was being picked up after school by Mr. and Mrs. Sparkman. He was a deacon in the Whitehaven Church of Christ, where our family attended church.

As I got into their car that afternoon in May, a news report was coming over the radio: "Elvis Presley was married this morning in Las Vegas." I started laughing. "That's a bunch of baloney—Elvis isn't married."

Mrs. Sparkman said, "I don't know, David. After all, your parents are out in Las Vegas, too."

When we got to Graceland, the phone was ringing. It was my mother.

"We just wanted to let you boys know. Elvis and Priscilla were married this morning."

Later that day, Elvis called and talked to all of us. He told us he was sorry that we weren't able to come to the wedding, but there was going to be a reception when they got home to Memphis, and we were all invited to that.

The first thing I said to him was, "What are you going to do about your movies?"

He laughed. "Well, David, we all have to settle down sometime!"

I knew that Elvis's movies usually involved him in love scenes with beautiful women, and I was sure that a married man couldn't make movies like that. As much as I cared for Priscilla, I figured that by marrying her, Elvis had put an end to his career.

I was wrong. There were several more movies, with several beautiful co-stars.

The summer of 1967 found him filming *Speedway* with Nancy Sinatra. We boys got to go with him, and we spent most of the summer at Elvis's Bel Air home. He would wake us up every morning at five o'clock and take us to the studio with him. We would watch them filming the race scenes, and we got to meet Nancy Sinatra and Bill Bixby. There was another girl there who had a small role, and I thought she was beautiful. She was a dancer named Terri Garr. I knew she would be a star someday.

MGM also was filming *Ice Station Zebra* on its lot that summer, so we got a firsthand look at how that movie was made. Elvis introduced us to Ernest Borgnine, Rock Hudson, and Jim Brown—a football hero of ours who had recently become an actor. We also got to meet Ronald Reagan, who was the governor of California.

Pretty soon, we got to believing that we had the run of the studio. Billy and I would ride around on our double bicycle, just looking at the various sets. One day, we came around a corner, and suddenly found ourselves in the middle of a war.

Boom! An explosion went off just behind us. Kablam! Another one in front of us sent a dust cloud swirling into the sky. All of a sudden, a soldier in camouflage was rushing toward us, aiming some vicious-looking weapon in our direction. We dropped the bike and prepared to run for our lives.

"Cut! Cut! What is going on here?"

A group of angry-looking people descended on us. (At least they were civilians and not carrying guns.)

"What do you kids think you're doing?" one of them yelled. Then, before we could even stammer out an answer, he turned to the woman beside him. "Who are these kids anyway?"

"We're Elvis Presley's brothers, sir."

Immediately, the man's mood softened. "Oh, you are?"

It turned out that we had bicycled right into the middle of a show called "Garrison's Gorillas," and we'd ruined an entire scene.

"Well, boys," the man said, reaching over to pat me on the shoulder, "if you want to stick around and watch the shoot for a while, feel free. But please watch where you're going with that thing."

We climbed back aboard our bicycle and pedaled shakily away, immensely grateful that Elvis Presley was our big brother. We both knew that that was the only thing that had kept those people from killing us!

Three

The Seeds of Rebellion

"David, what in the world is wrong with you, man?"

Elvis reached over and grasped my shoulder. He squeezed it, in a friendly, yet firm way.

"Don't you know you have to get along with people?" He stood up and went over to his window. He stood for a minute, looking out over the rolling Graceland landscape. "Those rules weren't put there to hassle you, man. They're for your own good."

"You don't worry about the rules," I shot back.

Elvis turned around to face me. "I don't have to. That's because I'm Elvis Presley—you're not." He was getting angry. "When you've made your first million, then maybe you can quit worrying about what other people think. But until then, you'd better learn how to behave."

"But it's—"

"And besides, I never, ever, got into a fight with one of my teachers." He sat back down beside me and put his arm around me. "David, listen to me. You have tremendous potential. Don't throw it away trying to be some sort of hot-headed rebel."

"But I'm tired of being hassled!"

"Hassled?"

"Yeah. I'm tired of everybody getting on my case, just because I'm your brother. I'm tired of school. And *most* of all, I'm tired of church. Church, church, church. That's all we ever do—go to church. Sunday morning, Sunday night, Wednesday night, Vacation Bible School. We might as well move into a church."

He stood up again. He gave me a disdainful stare and pointed down at me. "I don't want to hear you talking that way. Your momma's doing her best to raise you right, and you ought to appreciate it. You can *never* get too much of being in church."

For a second, I thought about asking Elvis why, if that were the case, he never bothered to step inside a church. But he was angry, and this definitely wasn't the time or place for a question like that.

Elvis was angry with me because I had just been kicked out of Harding Academy, a private school sponsored by the Churches of Christ, for fighting with a teacher. My parents had already informed me of their disappointment and anger. But Elvis apparently figured he could get through to me whereas they couldn't.

In a sense, he was right. The worst thing in the world, as far as I was concerned, was to have Elvis angry or disappointed in me. His approval meant everything. I idolized him, and I wanted him to be proud of me. But still, he didn't understand. People picked on me. They were out to get me. And when that happens, you feel like you have no other choice but to strike back.

I was in the seventh grade, the biggest, toughest boy in my class. I was already nearly six feet tall, and I weighed close to 150 pounds. I wasn't the type to go around looking for trouble, or to provoke a fight, but if trouble came my way, I was always ready for it.

On this particular day, I had been sitting in a classroom where we were grouped by tables. There were six of us at each table, and I didn't fit under the table as well as most of the other kids did. I really didn't mean to, but I started bouncing the table up and down with my knees.

"David Stanley! Stop bouncing the table please!"

I stopped for a moment. I was embarrassed and could feel my face redden as everyone turned to look at me.

Then, nervously, I started bouncing the table again. The teacher decided I was trying to show her up.

"Okay, young man, that's it!" She grabbed my arm and pulled me out of my chair. "Come with me, right now!"

When we got out into the hall, she pushed me—not that hard, but a push just the same—and nobody was going to push me. Before I could even think about it, I hauled off and slugged her on the jaw. She grabbed her jaw and screamed, and I took off running. I made it out the front door and headed across the street. I had no idea where I was going. I was just trying to get away from the school. Then I heard someone yelling, "Come back here."

I looked over my shoulder and saw the assistant principal chasing me, but instead of stopping, I ran faster. He tackled me in a field across the street from the school, and I started fighting with him. Eventually, with the help of reinforcements, he got me back to his office and called my parents from there. When Mom came to the school, he informed her that I was no longer welcome at Harding Academy.

Mom was totally at a loss. She just did not know what to do. It wasn't the first time I had been in this kind of trouble, but she had hoped that Harding would be just what I needed. After all, it was a school with a Christian emphasis, and that certainly couldn't hurt me.

My school career up to this point had been nothing to brag about. In third grade, I had run away from school twice because I didn't like my teacher. In fourth grade, there had been a similar incident and I had punched my teacher. But in the fourth grade, I was smaller and easier to handle.

I didn't want to be a troublemaker and thought that I tried very hard not to be one. But at the same time, I also believed that people were just against me. They didn't like me, and I didn't like them. My mother's response to all of my problems in school was to send me to various psychiatrists who tried to help me "work out my hostilities." They usually ended up telling her not to worry, that I was just going through a phase and that my aggressiveness was a sign of my creativity and intelligence.

Dad would lecture me when I got in trouble, but I always had the feeling that deep down inside he got a kick out of my attitude. After all, Elvis had always been a rebel, and Vernon himself had spent some time in jail during his younger days. More than once, I heard Dad and Elvis talking about me and laughing about something or other I had done. "That David is something else!" Elvis would laugh. Of course, to my face they always disapproved when I was in trouble and acted like they expected me to toe the line.

For instance, when I was eleven, I got caught trying to steal a case of beer from the corner grocery store. The man who caught me took me into his office and sat me down. "Who do you want me to call? Your father, or the police?"

"Call my father!"

When Vernon came to the store, the man started jumping all over me about what a terrible thing I had tried to do.

"Now wait a minute," Vernon said. "What the boy did was wrong. But don't you remember when you were a kid? Didn't you ever try to do anything like this?"

I was feeling pretty sure of myself. My dad understood. Everything was cool. But when he got me home, he really let me have it. That's the way it was. On the one hand, he understood, but on the other, he knew he couldn't let me get away with anything.

Vernon, like Elvis, paid lip service to my mother's religion. He agreed that we belonged in church, although he never went himself. He seemed to have the attitude, at that time anyway, that religion was for women and children.

My mother was a very devout woman. She read her Bible faithfully, and she prayed every day. She made sure we were in church. But we never really talked about God.

I was torn, because I had spent enough time in church that I knew the Bible. I knew the difference between right and wrong. But I also wanted to be cool, like Elvis.

In 1963 I had gone forward at the end of a service to profess my faith in Christ and make a decision just to get Mom off my back. But at that time I felt the Lord was calling me to become a preacher. I practiced preaching when nobody was around, mimicking the style of C. W. Bradley, who was the preacher at Whitehaven Church of Christ. But that idea eventually faded. And now here I was an outcast. Told I couldn't return to Harding Academy.

My parents finally decided that the best thing to do was to send me off to military school. It would teach me responsibility—help make a man out of me.

It didn't take long before I decided it was going to *kill* me! If I didn't like living by the rules, I was most definitely in the wrong place. I had to learn to keep my bed and locker in tip-top shape. I had to learn to stand at attention and salute and say, "Yes, Sir," and, "No, Sir," to people I didn't care for. But the thing I hated above everything else was marching. We marched all the time! We marched before class, we marched after class, and sometimes we even marched in between classes.

We marched until I just knew I couldn't march anymore. Then I had an idea. I looked around until I found a nice, heavy brick. This was going to be painful, but it would be worth it if it got me out of this place and back home where I belonged.

The next morning I got my opportunity. I was alone in the barracks. I sat on the edge of my bed, holding the brick in my right hand. I closed my eyes . . . and brought the brick down hard on my right knee, but not hard enough. It hurt, but it didn't do much in the way of damage. I was going to have to grit my teeth and try it again. I bit my upper lip, took a deep breath, and brought the brick down on my knee with all my might. The pain was tremendous, as I felt my knee give way. Somehow, I kept from crying out.

I tossed the brick out the window. Then I lay down on the floor and began screaming in agony.

When people came running to my rescue, I told them I had fallen out of bed. I don't know if anyone believed me, but my plan worked. I wasn't fit for military school with a bum knee, so I was sent home. But not before I had had a second surgery on the knee—the same knee I had injured playing football two years earlier.

My parents decided to give me another shot at public school, enrolling me in Whitehaven Junior High. I was determined not to blow it this time. I tried my best to get along with people, even the teachers. The next two years were among the best, or at least the most productive, I ever spent in school. I got decent grades, I cooperated to the best of my ability, and I tried to stay out of trouble. But I was still simmering beneath the surface, an explosion waiting to happen.

Meanwhile, back at Whitehaven Church of Christ, I was also trying hard. Or at least I thought I was. I had made several close friends in the church, and we would take turns spending the night at one another's houses, going to movies together, and things like that. But even then, church was not much more than a social club, a place to go to see my friends. And my concept of God was a Big Brother figure who kept tabs on all my mistakes. I thought I had to walk the chalkline—get baptized, don't chew, drink, smoke, dance, or lust—and I'd be all right.

I believed in God, but I was more afraid of Him than anything else. Even during the years when I was on tour with Elvis, I always believed God was there, watching me, noting everything down on His gigantic scorecard. Just about every night, I would pray, "Dear Lord, forgive me for my sins. If I die tonight, don't let me go to hell." I figured that if I prayed that prayer I had all the bases covered!

I was getting a good foundation at Whitehaven Church of Christ—learning the Ten Commandments, the Twenty-third Psalm, the Lord's Prayer, and other passages from the Bible—but I never did develop a relationship with the One who had inspired all of those passages.

Then one Sunday morning as we were leaving the church, two of the deacons approached me.

"David, we want to talk to you for a minute."

"What about?"

"Don't you think your hair is getting a little long?"

"Yeah. Maybe. But I like my hair this way."

"Do you think a Christian ought to go around with his hair like that?"

The other deacon nodded in agreement. "You really ought to get your hair cut, son!"

I could feel my face turning red, but then I saw my mother and told the deacons I had to go.

I was so angry, I was shaking. How *dare* they talk to me about my hair? What I did with my hair was none of their business. If I wanted to paint it polka-dot, that was nobody's business but mine.

I knew that Mom would be on my side. I was shocked when she wasn't. "David, your hair *is* getting awfully long. I think you should get it cut." Then she told me that one of the deacons had also talked to her about my hair.

"I don't care what anybody says," I shot back. "My hair is none of his business. He's just jealous because he doesn't have any hair of his own!"

As I got in on the passenger's side of the car, I slammed the door as hard as I could to show how angry I was.

"David!"

I had heard this sort of talk before. Every once in a while, someone at church would say that I was looking a little shaggy or ask me if I was ashamed of my ears. Even though I hadn't especially appreciated those remarks, I had always thought they were made in jest. But now, Mom was telling me that the deacons were ordering me to get my hair cut. Who did they think they were?

"They can forget it. I'm not going to get a haircut!" I slouched down in the seat as Mom pulled out of the church parking lot and onto Elvis Presley Boulevard.

"David Stanley! I will not put up with this attitude. What kind of an example do you think you're setting? How do you think the Lord must feel with you going around looking like that?"

I pulled down the sun visor and looked at my reflection in the mirror. My hair was long, but no longer than most of the guys at school wore theirs. Long hair was in style. Why couldn't older people understand that?

"Jesus' hair was longer than mine!"

"That can't be true, because the Bible says it's shameful for a man to have long hair."

"I don't care what the Bible says!"

I didn't realize that the deacons had put poor Mom on the spot. All I could see was that for some reason they had decided to gang up on me, and instead of defending me, Mom had joined the enemy.

We were locked in a classic struggle of, "Yes, you will"/"Oh, no, I won't," and neither one of us was about to give an inch. By the time we got home, the argument had escalated into a full-scale war.

I slammed the door as I got out of the car.

"Not only won't I get my hair cut," I yelled, "I am never going back to that church!"

Mom glared at me, her blue eyes flashing with anger.

"You get in that house," she shook her finger at me, "and you go to your room. And you stay there until I tell you to come out!"

"I'll go to my room!" I shouted back at her. "But I'll never go back to that stupid church. I hate it!"

"Go to your room. Now!"

"You can take your stupid church and. . . ." I slammed the

door so Mom wouldn't hear the rest of the sentence.

I went over and picked up a Bible from my dresser and threw it across the room. Then I punched the bed with my fist and flopped down on it.

I stared at the Bible. It had landed open, upside down, with the pages scrunched up underneath the cover. I picked it up and began ripping handfuls of pages out. I kept going until I had ripped the entire book into little pieces. When I was finished, I opened the door and called to Mom, saying I needed to talk to her for a minute.

When she came to the door, I was waiting with the pieces of my Bible. As she came down the hall, I threw them out in front of her.

"This is what I think of your stupid church!" I said defiantly.

Then I slammed the door in her face, and locked it.

Mom didn't know what to do. She didn't yell or threaten me. But I thought I heard her crying, and I'm sure her heart was broken. I was fifteen years old, much too big to spank, and what I had said was true. If I didn't want to do something, nobody could make me do it. I never again set foot inside the Whitehaven Church of Christ.

I think Mom must have felt a little guilty over the fact that she had divorced my dad to marry Vernon Presley. And every time I did something wrong, no matter how large or small it was, she immediately began thinking it was because of the divorce. The divorce had scarred me, she thought, and that's why I acted the way I did. The fact that I had now turned my back on church, and therefore, in her estimation, on God, was almost more than she could bear.

Once again, Elvis tried to come to the rescue. He told me how much I needed to be in church and how what I was doing was hurting my mother. But I told him that I had simply had enough of church, I wasn't going back, and there wasn't anything he could do about it. When he realized I felt that strongly about it, he didn't bring it up again.

If anyone knew how it felt to be criticized for being different, Elvis did. He had told me that when he was a teenager people often laughed at him and said hurtful things to him because they thought he dressed funny, and because of his long, bushy sideburns. When he was in high school, a group of bullies once ganged up on him in a rest room. There were five of them against Elvis, and they were going to cut his hair. They were trying to push him up against a wall when Elvis's friend Red West came along, and they all backed down.

That was the same sort of thing that had happened to me in the third grade at Graceland Elementary. When Elvis told me that story, it strengthened the bond between us. We both knew how it felt to be misunderstood and mistreated.

And if the church was going to treat me that way, I wanted nothing more to do with it or its moral standards.

I began smoking and drinking beer—just enough to show that I was hip. As far as drugs were concerned, I knew some guys who had tried them, but I didn't want anything to do with them. I knew that a couple of guys at Hillcrest High School, where I was in the ninth grade, had been arrested for selling marijuana. They would put it in one of those little matchboxes and call it Memphis Blue. I had gone to some parties where the kids were smoking pot, but I tried to stay away from it.

Then one day Rick and I, along with a friend named Bobby, were cruising around town, looking for something to do. Rick was driving and I was in the backseat. Rick pulled out one of those scary little matchboxes.

"Hey, man, let's smoke some grass!"

I knew Rick had tried marijuana, but I was still shocked that he had some with him.

"No, man. We can't do that!"

"Aw, come on," Rick pleaded, "don't be a jerk. It's not gonna hurt you."

Bobby turned to me. "Yeah, David. It's about time you learned to live a little."

We pulled off the road, into a city park. Rick rolled a joint and lit it. Then he handed it to me. Well, maybe it wouldn't hurt me. I took a deep drag. Nothing happened. I took another. Again nothing happened.

"Hey, Rick, he's gonna smoke the whole thing," Bobby said.

"Hand that up here!" Rick grabbed for the joint. I still didn't feel anything. Then all of a sudden I started laughing—and I couldn't stop. In the front seat, Rick and Bobby started laughing, too. We were all laughing hysterically, while trying at the same time to shush one another up. I had a wonderful feeling of euphoria. I also felt that everyone else in the park was looking at us and knew what we were doing.

I loved pot, and before long I was smoking just about every day. I would smoke before school in the morning and go to school stoned. I thought the pot was sharpening my senses. For instance, when I had been smoking, music was intensified, and I could hear many things I couldn't hear when I was straight. Food tasted better, like it had more flavor.

Everyone in my group was smoking dope. Then some of us went on to bigger and "better" things. One day, a friend turned me on to something he called "windowpane"—otherwise known as LSD. He told me it would open up a whole new world for me, so I took two hits of it.

I was at home, tripping out, hallucinating, and feeling totally weird when the phone rang. It was Elvis, saying he had rented out the Memphian Theater that night, so why didn't we come over there and see the film *A Clockwork Orange* with him and some of his friends.

"Sure, man!"

After I hung up the phone, I started worrying about it. What would Elvis think if he saw me like this? I went and found Rick.

"Rick, I can't talk to Elvis. I'm on drugs!"

"Don't worry about it. You'll be fine. Just be cool."

But at the theater, I wasn't fine. I was freaked out, and

even though I was trying to control myself, I was acting strangely. Elvis kept laughing at me. "David . . . the movie's good, but it's not *that* good."

When my behavior got worse instead of better, Rick finally told him that I had taken some LSD.

Elvis was furious, and he started yelling at me. But when he saw that I was too stoned to comprehend much of what he was saying, he told Rick to take me home.

The next day, he called and asked me to come over to Graceland; he wanted to talk to me. When Elvis was really angry, he had a way of looking at you that could just about make you wither up. His eyes would get cold and hard, and it was impossible to look him in the face.

I sat on the sofa in the den and hung my head, while he let me feel the full force of his anger.

"Listen, David . . . I don't want to *ever* hear of you taking acid again. Do you understand me?" He paced back and forth in front of me.

"Yes, sir."

"I'm not messing with you. If I ever catch you pulling a stunt like that again, I'll kick your butt—and kick it good!"

I didn't say anything. I knew better than to respond.

But Elvis wasn't through yet. "I don't understand how you could do that." His voice softened, "I'm telling you, David, if you don't stay away from those drugs, they are going to really mess up your life." He shook his fist in my face. "And if I ever catch you doing anything like this again, *I'll* mess up your life, first."

I looked up at him and nodded, letting him know that I understood what he was saying.

"So we understand each other?"

"Yes, sir."

"Then get the hell out of here. I'm so disappointed in you, I don't want to look at your face."

Elvis could be mean and sarcastic when he was angry. And even though I was already bigger than Elvis, I wasn't about to tangle with him. I'd seen enough to know that he was plenty tough. Besides, I felt terrible because he was disappointed in me. His approval was tremendously important.

As I left that day, I heard him mumbling something about rounding up all the pushers and having them shot. Elvis was vehemently against drugs. Even in his later years, when he was taking tremendous amounts of medication, he always justified it by the fact that his doctors prescribed them for him, and they wouldn't have prescribed them unless he really needed them. He never considered himself a druggie or an addict. To him, druggies and addicts were contemptible.

As I drove away from Graceland that day I knew there was only one thing to do: I had to make sure that Elvis didn't find out about my drugs. I certainly wasn't about to give them up!

*   *   *

Over the next year, my rebelliousness increased, and I became known around Hillcrest High as a guy you didn't mess with. One of my best friends, Jimmy Marberry, was a Golden Gloves boxer, and Jimmy and I didn't take any guff from anyone. We spent most of our time seeing what mischief we could get into.

By this time, Elvis was really sold on motorcycles. We would get out in the middle of the night and head down Highway 51 South as fast as we could go, and that usually meant speeds in excess of a hundred miles an hour. Elvis was stopped several times for speeding, but as far as I know, he never got a ticket.

He would always be "sincerely" contrite and apologetic. "I'm sorry, officer. I had no idea I was going that fast!" "Well, try to take it a little easier, Mr. Presley." "I sure will. Thank you, officer." But as soon as the police were out of sight, we'd be back up to a hundred miles an hour and sometimes faster. At that time, I was riding a 750 Honda with blown jets and a Hooker header. Elvis was always yelling at me to, "Turn it down! Turn it down!" But if I wasn't out riding with Elvis, you could most likely find me riding with Jimmy.

Jimmy and I were like brothers. We shared our deepest secrets. And Jimmy was probably the only one who could talk to me when he thought I was getting too heavily involved in drugs.

He might have smoked some grass from time to time, but that was it. I started calling him "the preacher" because I thought he was much too concerned about my welfare. That part of my life was nobody's business. Not Elvis's and not Jimmy Marberry's.

My other best friend was Jackie Stovall, whose family held a special place in Elvis's heart from a time before he became a star. Back then Elvis had hoped to be an electrician. He went to several banks in the Memphis area, trying to borrow some money to help him get started in business. But because Elvis had nothing to offer in the way of collateral, he couldn't get the loan. Until, that is, he went to the bank where Jackie's grandfather, Jack D. Stovall, Sr., served as vice-president. Mr. Stovall believed in Elvis and gave him the money he was seeking. Elvis never forgot the one man who believed in him when nobody else did. When he hit it big, all of his money went into that bank. When it came time for Jack Stovall to retire, Elvis told him he wouldn't trust his money to anyone else, and so he set Stovall up in his own business, handling only Elvis's account.

I first met Jackie around 1962, when Elvis developed an interest in flying remote control airplanes. Jackie's father had a special airplane that he had built and then sold to a local hobby shop. He was especially proud of that airplane and wanted to make sure that whoever bought it would take good care of it.

When Mr. Stovall found out that Elvis had bought it and that he had quite an interest in such airplanes, he and Jackie came to Graceland to talk to Elvis. We all sat in the living room, while Jackie's father showed Elvis some of the special features he had built into that particular airplane.

"You know, Elvis, you got a real bargain here. Three hundred and fifty dollars for this airplane is a terrific deal!"

Elvis leaned back on the sofa and laughed.

"Three hundred and fifty dollars—I paid a thousand for it!"

"A thousand!" Jackie's dad nearly dropped the airplane. "That crook!"

Jackie's father was so angry, he wanted to go down to the hobby shop and punch the owner out. But Elvis just kept chuckling. "Don't worry about it. I'm used to it. When they see me coming, they figure it's a chance to make a little extra money. That's just the way it is."

"But it's not right."

"That's what happened with Graceland. The owners wanted fifty thousand for it. Then, when they found out I was the one interested in buying it, all of a sudden, the price went up to a hundred thousand."

"Why don't you do something about it? Don't let people take advantage of you like that!"

Elvis shrugged. "Shoot . . . I got plenty of money. Don't see any reason I should get all worked up about it."

Jackie and I didn't become really close friends until the late sixties or early seventies—after Elvis's daughter, Lisa Marie, was born. I spent a lot of time playing with her, riding her around in golf carts, and playing hide-and-seek. Often Jackie would be with me, and when he was, we liked playing hide-and-seek best of all. That's because we had some pretty good hiding places where we could sit and smoke a couple of joints while Lisa was looking for us.

Even as a little, tiny girl, Lisa was always asking her father to have me play with her: "Daddy, get David to take me for a ride." "Daddy, ask David to play a game with me." I think Elvis was a little jealous that she was always asking for me, but at the same time, I was one of very few people he trusted with her safety. And he trusted me with her because he knew how much I loved her.

Lisa loved to ride in the golf carts, and the faster the better. She was just like her daddy, always wanting to go faster, faster, faster! "Come on, David, you're not going fast enough!" The closer we came to disaster, the more she liked it, and the more she laughed.

Lisa got away with an awful lot. She was her daddy's pride and joy, and she knew it. If we didn't do what she wanted, she would threaten to tell her daddy, and none of us wanted to be in the position of forcing Elvis to choose between us and her. We figured we wouldn't have a chance.

One evening, Jackie and I were playing hide-and-seek with her. And, as was often the case, we were both stoned out of our minds. Lisa had a squirt gun, and when she found us she squirted Jackie right in the eye.

Suddenly, Jackie jumped up and started rubbing at his eye as hard as he could. "Ow! What is that? What do you think you're doing?"

Little Lisa stuck out her lip and aimed the gun at me.

"Anything I want to do. And I want you to get mad!"

I got the gun away from her before she could take a shot at me. It was filled with dishwashing liquid!

Jackie and I were hopping mad, but we knew she was right. She could do anything she wanted to do, and there wasn't a thing we could do to stop her.

The next day, Jackie came up to Graceland again. When Lisa saw him, she went into the kitchen and got a fried chicken leg. She came back and held it out to Jackie.

"Here, Jackie, this is for you."

"What's this for?"

"Because I'm sorry about last night."

I was shocked, because that was the first time I had ever seen her apologize to an outsider—someone who wasn't a member of the family—for anything.

She very seldom felt the need. And what I didn't realize was that my attitude was pretty close to hers. She was Elvis

Presley's daughter. I was Elvis Presley's brother. We both felt that made us privileged characters, and if you didn't like it, that was your problem.

But Lisa was only a little girl. She hadn't yet learned the importance of the Golden Rule, that you must always treat others as you would want them to treat you. As for me, I was rapidly approaching manhood, but I had left the Golden Rule, along with all the other moral laws, way back there in the dust of the past, along with my mother's church—the Whitehaven Church of Christ.

Four

At Home With the King of Rock 'n' Roll

I was becoming increasingly comfortable in my role as Elvis Presley's brother. After the incident that got me kicked out of Harding Academy, I had become more certain of who I was and where I was heading. Someday, I would be working full-time for Elvis, making bundles of money and living the good life.

But while I was becoming more and more confident about the direction of my life, Elvis was asking more and more questions about the purpose of his own—especially about the reasons for his tremendous popularity.

The years between 1963 and 1968 were particularly troublesome ones.

Elvis had made more than thirty motion pictures since the middle fifties, when he had made his first movie, *Love Me Tender*. He was currently locked into his second five-year contract with MGM, a contract that called for Elvis to star in three movies every year. Elvis had entered the acting profession with enthusiasm and optimism. He took acting seriously and wanted to make quality motion pictures. He worked hard, hoping to win international recognition for his skills as an actor.

But over the years, he had become increasingly disillusioned. The studio was content to churn out movies that had nothing going for them except Elvis's appearance in them. Most of the movies did very well at the box office, but still Elvis longed for a role that would show the world he could handle more than the simple boy-meets-girl stories he was always being handed by the studio. Not that all of Elvis's pictures were bad. Some of them were interesting, entertaining pictures, but none were of Academy Award quality. By the late sixties, Elvis's hopes of being a respected actor had been replaced by the frustration of being locked into a long-term contract that was preventing him from doing what he really wanted to do.

Elvis's movies always included several songs, but he was not especially pleased with the songs he was being asked to sing. Record sales were still substantial and money continued to pour in, but he had not had a number 1 single since "Good Luck Charm" in early 1962, and he recognized that most of the songs he was being offered were not of lasting quality.

Beyond that, the music world was undergoing drastic changes, and Elvis's one-picture-after-another movie schedule had kept him from playing a more active role in the creative explosion that was taking place. Beginning in 1964, with the Beatles' arrival in the United States, new and immensely talented musicians were popping up everywhere. There was a new excitement that had not been felt since Elvis himself had burst upon the scene in 1956, and Elvis wanted to be a part of it.

Even though he presented a public attitude of nonchalance and overconfidence, the truth was that he really did not understand why he was so popular. He felt, deep down inside, that his popularity was a gift, and he didn't want to squander it singing songs like "Do the Clam."

Elvis was always quick to get angry, and that's one thing

you had to understand if you were going to be around him much. He was liable to jump all over you for the smallest reason, although he would always feel bad about it later and apologize. Then he would try to make it up to you by buying you something: a motorcycle, a car, a house. On one such occasion, he had even attempted to give me a check for one million dollars.

"Elvis, I can't take this!"

"David, I really want you to have it. I love you, and I want to prove it to you."

"You don't have to prove anything to me, man. I love you, too ... and I don't want your money!"

When he insisted on giving me the check, I tore it up. That was because I had seen too many other people who were only interested in Elvis for what they could get out of him. I wanted him to know that I loved him because he was a terrific big brother, and not because he was a famous entertainer.

Yes, Elvis had always had a hair-trigger temper, but that was especially true during those latter years of his movie career. He absolutely detested most of the movies he was making.

I remember one occasion, on the set of *Speedway,* when his frustrations boiled over. One day, late in the afternoon, the director told Elvis he wasn't playing a scene right. I don't remember now exactly what the director wanted Elvis to do, but Elvis didn't like it one bit.

He stormed over and glared at the director. "Where do you get off telling me how to act! You don't know what you're talking about! If you don't like what I'm doing, you can take this stupid movie and shove it!" He kept up the tirade for a good five minutes, while the poor director just stood there and took it. I was just twelve years old, but I was terribly embarrassed for Elvis. I thought he was acting like a spoiled child.

That night at the dinner table, he tried to explain what had happened.

"Guess I got a little carried away today, didn't I?" He laughed, as if the whole thing were a joke. Then he got serious. "David, I'm just sick to death of movies!"

"Why?" I couldn't believe that anyone would be tired of starring in movies.

"I'm sick of singing to dogs and dancing with chimpanzees and all the other stupid things they have me doing. I just want to get back on the stage."

Elvis's frantic life-style didn't allow him much time to really think about the situation, but at Graceland, he would sometimes retreat to the quietness of his Meditation Gardens. In this place he could take a few moments to try to regain his perspective. On a few occasions I went and sat there with him, to listen while he talked about his understanding of the meaning of life.

One time we were sitting in the gardens just as the sun was going down. In the middle of the gardens there was a statue of Jesus—a very dramatic statue in a long, flowing robe. Elvis had seen the statue dozens of times before, but for some reason on this particular evening he seemed to be fascinated by it. He sat on a bench, leaning forward, just looking at that statue for the longest time.

I sat beside him, waiting for him to reveal what was on his mind. I knew he was bothered about something and that he needed someone to talk to. Finally, he spoke.

"Jesus Christ— " he held out his hand toward the statue as he said it—"the Son of the living God."

I nodded. I believed that Jesus was the Son of God.

"He was really something," he continued. "He healed the sick, raised the dead . . . and everywhere He went, crowds of people followed Him."

I nodded again, wondering where he was going with this sort of talk.

"Even today, two thousand years later, people still talk about the wonderful things He did. He wasn't like any other man; He was different."

Elvis sat back and looked up into the clear Tennessee sky.

"David," he said, "I know who He was ... but who am I? What makes *me* different?"

I was trying hard to think of some reply, but nothing that made any sense would come to me. I was just a boy and had no idea how to respond. So I didn't.

"You know me. I'm your brother ... I'm just a regular man. But I'm Elvis Presley. Why do people react to me the way they do?"

Having said that, he went back to contemplating the statue of Christ. We sat there for probably another fifteen or twenty minutes without speaking. By that time, night had fallen, so we got up and went back into the house.

Elvis's restlessness and dissatisfaction during that time was compounded by the fact that he was about to become a father. All through Priscilla's pregnancy, Elvis had been excited and nervous. He was absolutely delighted that he was going to be a daddy, from the first moment he found out. But at the same time, he was frightened. What kind of father would he be? What sort of wisdom and knowledge would he be able to give to a child?

My brothers and I all *knew* that Priscilla was going to have a boy. We were wrong.

On the afternoon of February 1, 1968, Lisa Marie Presley was born. That evening, we all went to the hospital to see Priscilla and her new baby. Elvis was beside himself with joy. He was positively glowing! Everyone was happy, and I remember telling Priscilla how much I loved and appreciated her.

Later that night, Elvis called the family together. He wanted to let us know how good he felt and how happy he was that he had a beautiful baby daughter.

We sat in the living room with Elvis as he celebrated by puffing on a small cigar.

"You know," he said, "God has been very good to me. He's given me wealth ... and fame ... a beautiful wife ... and a terrific family. I have three wonderful brothers, and now I have a beautiful baby girl.

"She has perfect little hands and perfect little feet! She's just incredible!" He looked up as if to thank the Lord for all his good fortune.

Nobody else spoke. We were all just enjoying his excitement.

"I should have stayed in church. I should have been a preacher. That's the only way I could ever repay God for all He has given to me!"

Elvis was flying high that night. He had a feeling that this was to be his year, a turning point in his career. And, sure enough, in 1968 Elvis's career did take a dramatic upswing. I was about to see firsthand what had made Elvis Presley such a star in the first place.

*   *   *

Elvis was nearing the completion of his contract with MGM, and he was eager to once again perform his music before live audiences. But at the same time, he was afraid. He hadn't performed in public in over seven years. Back then, he had left 'em screaming for more. But that had been so long ago, when he was just a youngster. At thirty-three, Elvis was worried that perhaps he was over the hill. Would people still like him? What if they didn't?

After all, the world did not belong to Elvis Presley anymore. It belonged to John Lennon and Paul McCartney, to Mick Jagger and Jim Morrison. Elvis was dying to prove he was still the king of rock 'n' roll. But even he wasn't really sure that he still deserved the title.

Then the NBC television network, in conjunction with the Singer Company, made him an offer to star in his own television special. It was exactly what he needed. It would give him a chance to sing some of his biggest hits of years gone-by, plus some new songs—good songs—that would be written especially for the show.

The show would be taped in the summer, but not televised

until December, when it would be presented as a Christmas special. For several weeks leading up to the taping, the special was the foremost thing on Elvis's mind. He wanted to be better than good—he wanted to be great. He worried about it constantly. He tried to hide his fear the same way he always did, with his sense of humor. But with Elvis, you could usually tell how serious a situation really was by how many jokes he made about it. He knew that if he failed in this endeavor, he would be painted as a has-been, a relic of the past.

During the show, Elvis was on stage with four musicians he had known and worked with for years—Charlie Hodge, D. J. Fontana, Scotty Moore, and Alan Fortas. Their presence was a calming influence on Elvis, who, to put it bluntly, was scared! For the one-hour special, four hours of taping was done in front of two different audiences. It was a grueling ordeal that left Elvis physically and emotionally exhausted. But at the same time, he came away with a sense of exhilaration. The audience had loved him and he knew it.

"They still like me!" he said as he came off the stage. He said it with a sense of wonder, as if he really couldn't believe it or understand why.

But the positive reaction of the live audience didn't really prove anything. What would the American public think? How many people would even bother to watch? The show wasn't scheduled to air until December 3. That gave Elvis another five months to worry about it. He wasn't as worried as he might have been, though, because he knew the final product was in the capable hands of producer Steve Binder. He also knew there were some terrific new songs in the show. Songs like "If I Can Dream" and "Memories."

Still, when December 3, 1968, finally rolled around, it was a pretty nervous family group that gathered in front of the television set at Graceland to watch the show. But before the show was on five minutes, we all knew it was going to be a big hit. Dad kept slapping his knee and shouting, "That's my boy!"

Elvis, too, was jubilant. It was even better than he'd expected.

When the ratings came out, they, too, were even better than any of us had dared to hope for. The Christmas special, simply titled "Elvis," was the highest rated special for the entire year. When "If I Can Dream" was released as a single, it raced quickly up the charts, falling just short of *Billboard* magazine's Top 10. It was Elvis's highest charting record in over three years. And what made it even more exciting for him, as well as for the people at RCA, was that it was a "new" recording. He had done very well in 1965 with three songs—"Crying in the Chapel," "Easy Question," and "I'm Yours"—but all three had been recorded several years earlier. Elvis's latest records hadn't done nearly so well. Another song from the special, "Memories," also made it into the Top 40, and everyone was talking about Elvis's phenomenal comeback. Comeback? We all knew that he had never been away in the first place!

That was a great Christmas at Graceland. Everyone was in high spirits. Elvis and Priscilla were very much in love, and Lisa Marie was old enough to be excited about the holiday.

Christmases at Graceland were always fun. It was the one time of the year when the entire family got together. There would always be a beautiful Christmas tree, and the dining room table would be piled with an incredible number of presents.

On Christmas, Elvis liked to gather the family around the piano in the music room to sing Christmas carols. He loved some of the traditional favorites, like "Hark the Herald Angels Sing," and he made sure that everyone joined in. Elvis always sang those songs with a great deal of emotion and conviction. He really believed what he was singing.

But the best part was yet to come—Christmas dinner! Elvis's cook, Lottie, would concoct an amazing assortment of dishes and goodies, and Dad would always joke that he wouldn't be able to eat again for the rest of the year.

Elvis was especially excited that Christmas of 1968. Now

that the first Elvis special was history, he couldn't wait to start touring again. He decided that as soon as he finished filming *Change of Habit,* his thirty-first and last movie, he'd get back out on the road. Before he was able to do that, he recorded a song written by his friend Mac Davis. The song was "In the Ghetto." It shot straight to the top of the charts, becoming Elvis's first million-selling single in years. It was a beautiful song, but in the record business, beautiful songs don't always make it to the top. You have to be "hot" before most radio stations will play your records. If people don't hear your music, they don't buy it. And if radio stations don't play your music, nobody hears it. "In the Ghetto" proved that Elvis Presley was back at the top. Everywhere you went, you heard that song being played. The king had reclaimed his throne!

*   *   *

A few months later, in July of 1969, Elvis Presley opened at the International Hotel in Las Vegas.

While Elvis was rehearsing, the rest of the family flew to Hawaii for a short vacation. We flew back to Las Vegas in time for his opening on July 26. I was a month short of my fourteenth birthday, and I was totally astounded by Las Vegas. I had never seen anything like it. The entire desert was ablaze with neon lights; each hotel, each casino seemed anxious to outdo the next one.

What's more, this flashiest, showiest of cities had been completely taken over by Elvis, even before his first show there. Thanks largely to the efforts of Colonel Parker, everywhere you looked, you saw Elvis Presley—on billboards, posters, newspapers. The city of Las Vegas seemed to consist of flashing lights and pictures of Elvis. You couldn't turn on the TV or radio without hearing an upbeat commercial announcing that Elvis was in town.

The night before Elvis opened, he took us to Barbra Streisand's show. That was the first time I had ever seen a show like that, and Barbra Streisand was awesome. Still, I was not prepared for what I was going to see the following night. I'd seen Elvis performing in public way back in 1961. I'd seen him singing in his movies, and I'd seen the Christmas TV special. But I never knew my big brother could rock 'n' roll like he did that first night in Las Vegas!

When he first walked out on stage, the standing-room-only audience gave him an ovation that lasted several minutes. As Elvis stood there, waiting for the cheers to die down, I could feel the pride welling up within me. As far as I was concerned, they might as well have been cheering for me.

Then, suddenly, it was, "One for the money! Two for the show ..." and Elvis and the band were racing into "Blue Suede Shoes." Elvis was phenomenal, and so was his band. On the Christmas special it had been Elvis and his friends playing acoustic guitars and tambourines. In Las Vegas, Elvis was accompanied by an orchestra and chorus, complete with brass section and strings. It seemed as if the musicians anticipated every move Elvis made, and I was astounded at how Elvis could rock out. Even those "ancient" songs like "Don't Be Cruel" and "All Shook Up" sounded new and exciting! The audience loved it. They cheered and whistled and screamed as if they had never seen such a show—and they probably hadn't.

After the show that opening night there was a big party in honor of Elvis, and the place was packed with celebrities. Gregory Peck and Burt Lancaster were there. So were Tom Jones, Barbra Streisand, Wayne Newton, George Hamilton, and many others. I couldn't believe that all of these famous people had come to see my brother perform.

Backstage, Elvis was lying down on the sofa in his dressing room, trying to get a few minutes rest before joining the party. He was happy with the way the show had gone, but he was also exhausted. He had given the performance everything he had.

All I could say was, "Man! You really know how to rock!"
He chuckled. "Thanks, Dave-O."

"It was really groovy!"

"*Groovy?* That's a pretty heavy compliment. I guess that's the first time you've ever seen me perform, huh?"

"Well . . . the first time in a long time."

"David, what you saw tonight . . . that's the reason they call me the king of rock 'n' roll." He said it matter-of-factly, without a hint of boasting. And I knew it was true. If he could put on a show like that every night, he really *was* the king of rock 'n' roll.

For the next four weeks, Elvis packed the International Hotel twice a night. And every night, there was the same enthusiastic response and the universally favorable reviews.

Before he left Las Vegas, Colonel Parker had signed Elvis to a long-term contract. Elvis would play month-long engagements at the International Hotel every August and every February for the next five years.

And the fun was just beginning. By September of 1969, Elvis had hit number 1 on the charts with "Suspicious Minds." It was his first number 1 single in seven and a half years ("In the Ghetto" had peaked at number 3), and it was the second of four million-sellers Elvis would record within a year's time. His albums were selling well, too, and even some of the earlier ones were back on the best-selling charts. Elvis was every bit as popular as he had been back in 1956.

After his second appearance in Vegas, he headed out on his first national tour. The family was on hand in Houston when Elvis kicked off the tour by performing in front of eighty thousand people at the Astrodome. It was a thrill for me to even be at the Astrodome, and Rick and Billy and I went exploring the day of the concert.

Elvis seemed as impressed by it as we were. Before his concert, when he was getting dressed, all he could talk about was how big the Astrodome was.

"Can you believe this place?" he asked. "How in the world did they ever build this thing?"

I was amazed. Elvis was about to perform before an audience forty times the size of the ones he had been playing to in Las Vegas, but he didn't seem the least bit nervous. Instead he was making small talk about the Astrodome and carrying on like your ordinary, everyday tourist. But then, when he went to take a drink of water, I realized his hand was shaking. The king was nervous after all.

By this time, Elvis had decided to do everything right. If he was the king of rock 'n' roll, he should dress like the king of rock 'n' roll. He began wearing a succession of spectacular costumes. In Houston he wore a dazzling white jump suit with loads of pearls and fringe.

When it was time for the show to start, Elvis was driven into the middle of the Astrodome in a flashy convertible. When the crowd recognized Elvis, the roar was deafening. As the cheer continued, he was driven around the stadium so everyone could get a closer look. Then, it was into the same dynamic kind of show he had been giving in Las Vegas. Elvis may have been nervous before the show, but once he started performing, every hint of it disappeared. He was super, and the crowd went wild.

Elvis was on top of the world, full of life, and he was loving every minute of it!

Things were going well on the road, and they seemed to be going well at home, too. When he was home, he was a doting father. Lisa Marie was, beyond a doubt, the joy of his life. He spoiled her as much as Priscilla would allow him to—and he was probably more lenient with her because he was gone so much of the time. He knew he was missing some important events in his little girl's life, and he tried to make up for it by giving her everything she could possibly want.

Or, perhaps that was just another manifestation of Elvis's generous spirit. Elvis's family had been desperately poor when he was a child, and as an adult, whenever he saw anyone in need, he wanted to help. Whenever he would read in the newspaper about a family being burned out or evicted, he would have one of us call the editor to find out how he could help. He gave away thousands of dollars in that way.

One year, he bought nineteen Cadillacs for the members of his staff—all at once, from the same salesman. Imagine the commission that salesman must have received!

Elvis bought all of his Caddies from that dealer, and he was a very good customer. One time, he asked me to go with him to check out the new Cadillacs. We were in the showroom when a middle-aged black woman came in. She was neatly dressed, but her clothes were old, and she didn't look as if she were in the market for a new Cadillac.

The dealer was showing us the latest model, but Elvis interrupted him right in the middle of his sales pitch.

"I like this car . . . I'll take it. And give the keys to that woman over there. It's for her."

Naturally, when the woman found out what Elvis had done, she screamed and started hugging and kissing him. Her husband was standing outside, and when he saw her carrying on like that, he came in to see what was going on. He, too, was excited, and thankful. In talking to him, we found out that he had lost his job, and the family was in severe financial trouble.

Elvis called the dealer. "I want to buy another car for this gentleman."

A few minutes later, the couple's twenty-year-old son came in, and Elvis bought a Cadillac for him, too. Not only did Elvis buy the family three brand-new Cadillacs, but he bought them a house and furnished it and paid off all their outstanding bills!

That's the way Elvis was, especially during those high-flying days of the early seventies. When he was a child, growing up in a poor family, he dreamed a lot of big dreams. And once he was able to do it, he got a tremendous thrill out of making other people's dreams come true.

(Some people may wonder why I bothered to mention that the people he bought the Cadillacs for were black. Because, even though Elvis was a true Southerner, spending his younger years in Mississippi and Tennessee in the days of segregation and racial strife, he was never prejudiced. Some people have charged, in recent years, that Elvis was a racist "redneck." Nothing could be further from the truth. Elvis had nothing but the highest regard and respect for black people. I think that says something about his character.)

It was around this time that Elvis developed a passion for law and order. He had become increasingly angry over what he saw going on in the country. Talk of revolution was everywhere, and many of America's college campuses were plagued by violent protests. Elvis admired the creativity and the music of groups such as the Beatles, but he came to detest their antiestablishment views. Elvis always felt very strongly about his country, and he believed that much of the music of that day was simply anti-American. He was further angered by music that glorified the use of drugs.

Elvis had been crazy about guns for as long as I could remember. But now, the situation was becoming intense. He was beginning to see himself as a champion of justice, and he would often wear a gun.

He talked to me about being a narc at Hillcrest High School.

"David, these drug dealers are ruining our country. We have to do something about it!"

"Are you kidding me? You want me to get myself killed?"

"David, you could do it, man. You're the right age, you have long hair, and you're hip. You could make friends with these people. . . ."

He wasn't going to take no for an answer. I finally told him I would keep my eyes open and hoped he would forget about it. Every once in a while, though, he would bring it up again. I thought he was playing a very dangerous game, and I wasn't going to get myself into a life-threatening situation just to please him.

Elvis always had a large group of men around him: managers, bodyguards, hairdressers, musicians, "gofers." These men became known as the Memphis Mafia, and in 1970 Elvis was able to get the whole group deputized by the Shelby County, Tennessee, Sheriff's Department. Some of the men thought it was rather funny, but to Elvis it was deadly serious. He wanted it clear which side he was on.

Wherever he went, Elvis had friends in the police department. He loved to sit and talk police business, and he wound up with a large assortment of badges. In Denver, for instance, he held the honorary rank of captain. When one of his policeman friends died, Elvis showed up at the funeral in a full-dress uniform.

He also had a wonderful time serving as a one-man vigilante force for the Tennessee Highway Patrol. He had a black Ferrari, and sometimes at night when we would go riding, he'd get that thing up to 160 miles an hour. There wasn't anything around that could beat him. Just about every time I went riding with him, I wasn't sure if I would be coming back. When you're traveling down Highway 51 South at 160 miles an hour, the scenery flashes by in sort of a psychedelic blur, and all you can do is hang on!

He would put a blue light on top of that Ferrari, and we would go out cruising. When he saw someone breaking the speed limit, he would pull them over. Then he'd get out of his car and saunter over to his "victim."

"Excuse me, but you were going pretty fast, sir. I think you'd better slow it down a little bit."

"Yes, sir, Mr. Presley!"

If the offender were from out of state, Elvis's approach went something like this:

"Ma'am, we have laws around here that we're pretty particular about. And the speed limit is one of those laws. We'd appreciate it if you'd slow it down a little bit."

I can't remember anyone ever becoming angry or arguing with Elvis. Most of them loved the idea that they had been pulled over by Elvis Presley.

"Yes, sir, Mr. Presley. Thank you, I'll do what you say!"

You could see them laughing or looking at each other in amazement as Elvis would march back to the Ferrari, climb in, and speed away in search of other lawbreakers—not unlike the Lone Ranger galloping away on his faithful horse, Silver.

Nobody but Elvis could have gotten away with behaving like that. But all of the police in the Memphis area knew him, and if that was what he wanted to do, they let him. Besides, he wasn't hurting anyone, and if he caused a few people to drive more carefully, then he probably was doing some good.

In December of 1970, the highlight of Elvis's "career" in law enforcement occurred. He went to Washington and met with President Richard Nixon, who named him a federal narcotics agent. Of all his many badges, Elvis was proudest of that one. Elvis Presley: federal narcotics agent! I believe he was prouder of that than he was of all the gold records lining the walls at Graceland.

He must have shown me that badge five or six times, and each time I reacted with the same enthusiastic excitement.

Elvis took his authority seriously, too. He believed drug abuse was one of the greatest, if not *the* greatest, problems facing the United States.

He also took to wearing his gun more and more and expecting the other guys to wear guns, too. He had good reason, since there had been several threats on his life. And I'll have to admit, there were times when I was glad he had his gun!

One time Elvis, Dick Grob, and I were on a bus when it broke down. (Dick Grob had been a Palm Springs police sergeant before he came to work for Elvis as a bodyguard.) We had been to see the Memphis Grizzlies of the World Football League play and we were on the way home. Don't ask me why we were on the bus—it was just that Elvis decided he wanted to ride the bus for a change.

But when the bus broke down, Elvis was impatient. He didn't want to wait around while they tried to fix it. He wanted to get out and hitch a ride back to Graceland.

We got out of the bus and started walking down the street.

This was about eleven o'clock at night, and as I looked around, I realized that we were in a very bad part of town. We were right in the middle of what my friends and I called Murder City!

We saw a car coming down the street, an old beat-up Cadillac, so I stuck out my thumb. The car went past, then wheeled around and came back. There were a couple of men in the front seat, and one of them leaned out the passenger window to get a better look.

"Hey, Elvis!"

"We need a ride," I yelled.

"All right!"

The car swung around and came alongside us.

The first thing I noticed as I climbed into the backseat was the heavy odor of marijuana, and the floor was literally covered with empty beer bottles. Elvis's eyes met mine. Both of us knew we weren't in the safest situation. He reached his right hand up and patted the bulge under his left arm. He wanted me to know he was carrying his gun . . . just in case.

"I can't believe it! Elvis Presley!"

"Hey, Elvis," the driver teased him, "I sure could use a new car. What about it Mr. Presley?"

"Sure," Elvis answered. "I'll get you a new Cadillac. You go down to the dealer tomorrow and pick out anything you want."

The guys thought Elvis was kidding them, and they started joking about all the luxury items they were going to have added onto their new Caddies. We got to Graceland, and the guard at the Music Gate did a double take when he saw us riding in the backseat of that dilapidated old car, but then he waved us on through.

When we pulled up in front of the house, Elvis said, "I want you guys to wait out here for a couple of minutes. I'm going to get you something, and I'll be right back."

He went into the house, got his checkbook, and wrote out two checks for a couple hundred dollars. Then he took them out and gave them to the men for giving us a ride home.

I thought Elvis was crazy. I couldn't believe how much money he would just give away like that. But he seemed to know what I was thinking. "Aw, what the heck, David. It's only money."

* * *

In 1970, Rick had dropped out of high school to go to work full-time for Elvis. My mother was worried and upset because Rick was only sixteen, and she pleaded with him to stay in school. But when Elvis insisted he would see to it that Rick had a tutor and that he would be looked after, she finally agreed to let him go. I was jealous, because I wanted to go, too. But I was only fourteen and in the eighth grade.

Then, in January of the following year, Elvis was named one of the Ten Outstanding Young Men of America by the Jaycees. We went to the Memphis Holiday Inn, where he was going to be honored, along with the other recipients of this award, at a special banquet.

I was especially proud of him as he graciously accepted the award and concluded by saying that he would "just keep on singing my song."

After the awards ceremony, back at the hotel, Elvis called everyone into his room. He began handing out gold necklaces, which had the letters *TCB* and a lightning bolt on them. He explained that this meant "taking care of business as quick as lightning." There was one for Charlie Hodge, Joe Esposito, Lamar Fike, Red West, Sonny West, and on and on.

When he got through passing them out he looked at me. He could tell I was disappointed that he didn't have one for me.

"Someday, David, I'll give you one of these. But not now. When you're ready. And we'll both know when that day comes."

Five

On Tour: 1972–1977

February 23, 1972. I was at home in Memphis, and Elvis was calling long-distance from Las Vegas, where he was appearing at the Hilton Hotel. Elvis was still packing them in—and still getting rave reviews—but something was wrong. He sounded subdued, almost on the verge of tears.

We made small talk for a while, though I knew something serious was on his mind. But he caught me totally by surprise when he said, "Well, David, Priscilla told me today that she's leaving me. She's in love with someone else, and there's nothing I can do about it. I . . ." his voice trailed off. He was so choked with emotion, he couldn't finish the sentence.

"I'm sorry, Elvis. I'm really sorry." The words sounded so hollow. But what else could I say? I was sixteen years old—and suddenly very aware of my youth. I had no idea what to say to him at a time like this.

I listened to the silence for a minute or so. Finally, I said, "Elvis, I love you man. I really do. I hope you know that."

That was the first time I had ever been able to tell him how I really felt about him.

He sounded as if he were about to cry when he said, "I love you, too, David."

Priscilla leaving Elvis! All I could think was, *What a bummer for both Elvis and Priscilla. I know they love each other so much! How could this happen?*

Elvis was taken completely by surprise when Priscilla walked into his suite at the Hilton Hotel and told him she was leaving him for Mike Stone. He had always been sure that things were under control, that he was in charge, and now Priscilla was walking out and leaving him flat.

She added insult to injury when she admitted to Elvis that she'd been in love with Stone for more than a year. Not that Elvis had been faithful to Priscilla. I knew that when Elvis was on the road there were always plenty of women hanging around. Rick had been working for Elvis since 1970, and he had told me about all the chicks in Las Vegas. Elvis had even admitted to me, "Look, David, things are a little different than you've probably always thought." That was when I found out that Elvis's private life was not quite the same as his public image.

I was sixteen years old, and my reaction to this revelation was simply, "Far out!" I loved Priscilla and wouldn't have wanted to see her hurt for anything. She'd always been like a sister to me—one of my favorite people in the world. I simply didn't relate Elvis's behavior to pain for Priscilla.

But I know Priscilla knew what was going on, and so her marriage to Elvis had not been as dreamlike as she had tried to make it seem.

Furthermore, Priscilla never got to spend any quality time alone with him. It was never just the two of them going out for dinner, or spending a quiet evening at home in front of the fire. Priscilla always had to share Elvis with his Memphis Mafia. There were always five or six guys hanging around. When she married Elvis, it was like she married the whole group!

When Priscilla told him she was leaving, Elvis was deeply hurt. He really did love her, even though he wasn't taking his marriage vows seriously.

But by the time he got back to Memphis, his hurt had turned into anger.

"How could she have done this to me?" he would fume. "Leave me—Elvis Presley—for a two-bit karate instructor like Mike Stone? I ought to have that guy shot!"

Elvis was the dream of millions of American women. They proved it by throwing their room keys at him when he performed in Vegas. They wrote him thousands of letters every year, pledging their undying loyalty, offering to do anything he wanted, wherever and whenever he wanted. He was the king of rock 'n' roll. And yet the one woman he really wanted had rejected him—and rejected him for a man like Mike Stone. Stone was making perhaps twenty thousand dollars a year, compared to Elvis's millions. Elvis felt that Stone had nothing to offer Priscilla, while he had everything. The more he analyzed the situation, the more angry he became, and the more his ego was damaged.

What Elvis didn't realize was that Priscilla needed his love and attention much more than she needed material possessions. She needed some time alone with him, which she never was able to have. Like any other wife, she wanted her husband's affection, and his undivided devotion.

As time went by, I came to understand that this was something the king of rock 'n' roll was never able to give any woman, even the one he loved the most. And when Priscilla couldn't get what she really needed from Elvis, she found it somewhere else.

By summer, Elvis was getting ready to go out on another tour. He wasn't over Priscilla's leaving yet—not by a long shot—but one thing Elvis never did without was female companionship. By June, he was dating a beautiful girl named Lisa, who was a full-blooded American Indian.

On June 8, she and Elvis and I were riding horses around Graceland. Elvis was talking to Lisa and wasn't paying a great deal of attention to where he was going. I don't know exactly what happened, but something startled Elvis's palomino, Sun. The horse reared up, and Elvis went flying through the air. He hit the ground hard, and I was afraid he might really be hurt.

I knew that any injury would be serious, since Elvis was supposed to leave on his tour the very next day. I jumped off my horse and hurried over to him.

"Leave me alone!" he barked at me.

I stopped in my tracks.

"Just leave me alone!" he yelled again. "I'm all right." It was typical of Elvis not to want any help. He knew that Lisa had been riding horses practically all her life, and he didn't want to look bad in front of her.

Sun had run about twenty feet away and then stopped. He stood there watching us.

Elvis got to his feet and started walking toward his horse.

"Come on, Sun!" he called out in his most sugary voice. "Come on, boy . . . it's okay. It's all right."

Finally, the horse sauntered over to where Elvis was. And all of a sudden, Elvis punched that horse as hard as he could, right on the nose. He reached back and socked that horse with all of his might! Sun's legs buckled, but he didn't fall. He shook his head a couple of times and then took off running.

Elvis turned around toward us. "That'll teach him to throw me."

"Hey, man," I said, "I don't ever want to make you mad."

Later that afternoon, Elvis called me up to his room. He said he needed to talk to me alone.

"Dave, the time has come. You're going to work for me." He pulled out one of his *TCB* necklaces and placed it around my neck. When Elvis left on his tour, I would be going with him!

I had been hinting for months that I wanted to go on tour, but up till now I had never had any indication that Elvis was even listening to me. I was sixteen years old, had just finished the ninth grade at Hillcrest High School, and now I was heading out on tour with the king of rock 'n' roll. It was unbelievable!

Mom was not at all happy about my going off to be with Elvis. She pleaded with me not to go, but my mind was made up. She asked Elvis not to take me, but he had made up his mind that I was going with him and wouldn't be dissuaded. He told Mom that he would personally look after me. He'd keep me out of trouble, he'd pay me well, and it would be a great learning experience for me. Besides, it was only for the summer. By the time September came around, he would have me back in Hillcrest where I belonged.

Mom still wasn't convinced. She knew I shouldn't go, but it was everybody else against her. She had no choice, finally, but to give in and let me go. So on the morning of June 9, 1972, I climbed into Elvis's limousine, and we headed for the airport. As we pulled away from the house, I looked back and saw Mom kneeling in the driveway. Instead of waving good-bye, she was praying.

Poor Mom!

We went straight to the airport, where we boarded a private jet and flew off for New York City. Elvis would be giving three concerts at Madison Square Garden, and RCA was even planning to develop a live album from those concerts.

I felt like I was one of the "baddest dudes" around. What other sixteen-year-old was jetting around with Elvis Presley?

Elvis had given me very clear instructions. I was under the direction of Joe Esposito, and I was to do exactly what Joe told me to do. That was fine with me. Joe was a sharp guy, and of all the men in Elvis's entourage, he was the one I most admired. I knew, too, that Elvis admired and respected Joe. It was odd that the two of them were able to work so closely together, because they were so different. In many ways, they seemed to be complete opposites.

Elvis was the tall Southern gentleman with his roots in the country; Joe was a short, dark Italian from New Jersey. He was a flashy dresser, so we called him Diamond Joe. He was a natural leader, had a quick laugh, and did an amazing job of keeping things organized and running smoothly.

Despite their differences, Elvis and Joe had been close friends ever since they first met, while serving in the army.

I looked around the jet at the other men on board. We were a strangely diverse group, to say the least. There was little Charlie Hodge, who, like Joe Esposito, had met Elvis in the army. When Elvis finished his hitch and headed back home to Memphis, Charlie came with him. He was an excellent musician and played rhythm guitar on all of Elvis's tours.

Then there was Red West. Red had been Elvis's buddy since they attended L. C. Hume High School together back in the early fifties. And Red was one man you didn't want to mess with. He was tough and could be mean! He was a flag-waving, fight-at-the-drop-of-a-hat redneck.

His cousin, Sonny West, was exactly like Red, only more so. But they had to be tough and mean, because they were entrusted with guarding Elvis's life.

I'd known these men for twelve years, ever since I had come to Graceland, and they were to be my teachers—to show me the ropes of life on the road with Elvis.

Also on board was Larry Geller, who was Elvis's hair-dresser and his "guru." Geller was deeply into mysticism, Eastern religions, and so forth, and he had become Elvis's "spiritual" leader. Dr. George Nichopoulos (we called him Dr. Nick) was on hand to keep us healthy and to supply Elvis with the medication he needed for various ailments, plus vitamin B_{12} before shows. He was a gray-haired, distinguished-looking man who had had a successful practice in Memphis, but was making much more money working for Elvis.

There were several others on board, Dad and Rick among them, passing their time playing cards, reading magazines, just looking out the windows. These men would be spending the next several weeks together. It was no wonder that tempers sometimes flared and fistfights erupted. This was not a nine-to-five job, where you went home at the end of the day. When Elvis was on tour, they were on call twenty-four hours a day. They were together until they were sick of the sight of one another.

As we began our descent into New York, Rick looked out one of the windows. "All right," he yelled. "It's *party* time!"

Some of the guys started pulling out their little black books—the kind of books I had always heard about, but didn't know actually existed!

I was just sitting there, taking all this in. Joe Esposito came over and sat down next to me.

"Okay, David, buddy, we need to talk about a few things."

"Sure!"

"First of all, when we get out on the road like this, some of the guys like to have a little fun."

"Far out," I shrugged.

"And that's nobody's business but ours." He put his hand on my knee. "Anything that happens from now on, you—"

"Hey, don't worry about me," I interrupted him. "I'm cool."

"Good, good. Well, a couple of other rules. One, don't show Elvis any of the reviews about his concerts. Don't even talk to him about his concerts. If he asks you how you liked the show, feel free to tell him. But you wait for him to bring it up. Understand?"

I nodded.

"One other thing—and this is very, very important. Don't ever talk to the press. People are going to try to get information out of you, but you don't have anything to say."

"Okay. Yeah, I got it."

Joe leaned back and gave me his friendly smile. He punched me on the arm. "You're gonna do great, David. And you're gonna have the time of your life!"

I was sure of that. We were staying at the Hilton Hotel, right in the middle of Manhattan. I even had my own room.

There were pretty girls everywhere, dozens of them. I was starry-eyed. I had never been in New York before, except to change planes, and now I felt like the entire city belonged to me!

That night, before the concert, Rick and I were walking around backstage at Madison Square Garden. I saw a familiar figure leaning up against a post.

"Hey, aren't you George Harrison?"

He smiled. "I was last time I checked."

I extended my hand and he took it.

"You probably don't remember me," I said, "but I'm Elvis Presley's little brother. I met you—"

"Of course I remember. Memphis, back in sixty-five!" We talked for a few more minutes, and he told me about the concert he had just finished doing, to raise money for the starving people of Bangladesh.

"Where's Elvis?" he asked. "I'd like to say hello to him."

"Sure!" I said. "He'll be really excited to see you!"

Elvis was in his dressing room, with Joe Esposito and Larry Geller. Geller was putting the finishing touches on Elvis's hair. Harrison waited outside while I went in to tell Elvis he was there.

"Hey, Elvis, there's someone here to see you!"

Before Elvis could even answer, Joe Esposito was all over me.

"David! Elvis doesn't want to see anyone! Whoever it is, you tell them to get lost. . . . Elvis is getting ready to do a show, and he doesn't have time to sit and chat with people." Joe was angry that I had broken protocol, but Elvis decided to give me a break.

"Wait a minute, Joe. Don't be so hard on him . . . it's his first day on tour." He turned to look at his hair in the mirror. "Who is it, David?"

"George Harrison."

"Sure, tell him to come on in."

Elvis had mixed feelings about the Beatles, because he thought that much of their music had a negative influence, but George Harrison was all right. Harrison was a seeker of truth, just as Elvis was, and that gave them a special bond.

They talked for a few minutes, then it was time for us to go. It was nearly time for the show to start, so Rick, George Harrison, and I went and sat on the side of the stage. When Elvis came out, he was sizzling hot. It was one of the best shows I ever saw him do. He tore the place apart, and the twenty-two thousand people packed into the Garden went wild!

It continued that way for the rest of the weekend. The Garden was packed for every show, and Elvis set the place on fire. He was at his peak, physically and musically.

From New York, we headed for Evansville, Indiana, where Elvis was going to do one show. That was where I received my "initiation" into the group. As always, there were women hanging around, willing to do anything to get close to Elvis.

It was just after midnight, and Elvis had put on another great show. I had gone to my room, where I was planning to smoke a joint or two. One of the most exciting things about touring with this group was that it was so easy to get pot, cocaine, and other drugs. I was just lighting up when the phone rang. It was Elvis.

"David, get your butt down here. I need you . . . right away."

"Yes, sir!" I was trying hard to please him. I wanted him to know that he was right to bring me on this tour—that I belonged on the road with him.

I stuck the joint in my pants pocket and hurried to Elvis's suite. When I got there, the door was open, and I walked on in.

"Here he is, the star of the show!" Elvis was sitting on the sofa, holding a glass of Mountain Valley water. On his left were two gorgeous women, a long-haired, leggy blonde, and a petite redhead. On his right were two other women, just as beautiful. I tried not to look at them, because I was sure they "belonged" to Elvis. As I walked in the door, he put the champagne on the coffee table in front of him and started applauding.

Most of the guys were there, and they joined Elvis in applauding me. I could feel my blood pressure rising. It was like they were making fun of me, and nobody did that. Not anymore. But I was trying to control myself, because I didn't want to do anything to make Elvis angry.

He stood up. "Come on over here." The smirk on his face told me he was suppressing laughter. All the ladies were looking at me, and the leggy blonde on the far left giggled to herself. She, too, was in on the joke.

"David, buddy, this is indeed a solemn occasion." He said it seriously, as though he were officiating at a wedding or something. "We're delighted that you're with us . . . but we have to make sure you really belong."

Over in the corner, someone snickered.

"So, we have a little test for you."

"Ladies."

As he said the word, the four women got up off the couch and came over to me. The blonde took my left arm, the tall brunette took my right hand. The other two were touching my hair, running their fingers up and down my arms. All four of them were coming closer and closer, and I must have looked scared. I was.

"Ladies," Elvis said, "I give you a boy. Bring me back a man!"

As the five of us turned to leave, he called out, "I sure hope you can remember the way back to your room."

"Don't worry about that!" More laughter.

Well, after all, Elvis had promised my mother that he would watch out for me on the tour, that he would see to it that all my needs were met. And sure enough, sometimes unbeknown to Elvis, they were. I had access to all the dope I wanted. And there were women around to fulfill every sexual desire. What more could a sixteen-year-old boy want?

In fairness to Elvis, he really didn't know about the drugs, at least in those early days. Some of the guys in the group used drugs, but they tried to do it behind the boss's back. He didn't like it, and everybody knew it. In fact, Elvis's after-concert parties were usually pretty tame. We'd sit around drinking champagne, making small talk, and trying to find girl friends for the evening. Later on, we'd break out the booze and the grass, and things would really get going. But that would be without Elvis.

From Indiana, we headed to Chicago for several concerts. The first day we were there, someone called and said a bomb was going to go off during the show. The second day, another caller told us he was going to shoot Elvis during that night's performance.

I hadn't realized that Chicago was such a fun city!

I told Elvis about the bomb threat, and Red and Sonny jumped all over me. I wasn't supposed to worry Elvis by telling him things like that. He had enough things on his mind. It was their problem to worry about the nuts—and there were plenty of them out there.

They also told me not to worry about the gun threat. They kept their guns ready, and they kept their eyes open. If anybody tried to pull a gun on Elvis, they'd blow his head off before he had a chance to shoot. So I didn't tell Elvis about the caller who had threatened to shoot him.

But that night, midway through the show, someone in the audience set off a cherry bomb. BOOM! That thing sounded like a cannon going off.

Elvis immediately fell to the floor. "Oh, my God! I've been shot!"

Dad was sitting in the first row. He jumped up and yelled, "My son's been shot!" He was up on the stage with Elvis before anyone could stop him. I was sitting farther back, but I ran to the front as fast as I could and jumped up on the stage. Dad and I were both lying on top of Elvis, trying to protect him from his would-be assassin.

"What in the world are you doing?" Elvis asked in a surprised voice.

I said, "What do you mean, 'What am I doing?' You've been shot!"

"I haven't been shot!" He pushed us away.

"But there. . . ."

"I was joking—that was a firecracker. Now get off me!" By this time, he was laughing at our overzealousness.

"Elvis," I whispered as we all got to our feet and began dusting ourselves off, "we had a bomb threat yesterday."

"Yeah, I know. You told me."

"And then today," I informed him, "someone called and said he was going to shoot you!"

"What?" The smile disappeared. "Oh, God. Are you telling me the truth?"

"You picked the wrong night for that kind of joke," I said, indignantly. For the first time, I became aware that my act of would-be heroism had been witnessed by a packed audience.

Elvis switched on his microphone: "Hope you'll excuse me for a minute folks. We're having a family reunion up here!"

Dad and I were both just standing there, feeling embarrassed. Some of the band members were laughing, but the audience was astonishingly quiet. Perhaps they thought this was all part of the act.

"Well, gentlemen, I haven't been shot. But you can check me for bullet holes if you want to." Elvis started laughing again and shaking his head.

"David," he said, putting his arm around me, "you are absolutely crazy!"

Now, Elvis had always told me that he thought I would make a good bodyguard someday. I was big, a good fighter, and I wasn't afraid of anybody, even at sixteen. It was understood that one of my major duties on this summer tour would be to assist Elvis's other bodyguards, especially Red and Sonny West.

"Well, you told me you wanted me to be your bodyguard, and I don't want anything to happen to you!"

"David," he said as he put his hand on my shoulder, "you'll be the best bodyguard I ever had. But for now . . . get off the stage and let me finish the show!"

I didn't know what to think. Had I blown it by jumping up there on stage and interrupting the concert? But Elvis had said he was shot. How was I to know he was only joking?

After the concert, back at the hotel, I wanted to tell him I was sorry for messing up the show. He was lying down, trying to get a few minutes' rest before making his way to the usual party.

Elvis's performances always took a great deal out of him. He gave so much energy, that by the time the show was over he felt like he had been running up and down a basketball court all night. And the costumes he was wearing these days, with their pearls, diamonds, gold braids, and so on, often weighed in at twenty-five pounds or more. It was always a source of amazement that he could do two concerts in a single night, but he often did.

"David." He swung around on the couch and sat up as he saw me enter the room. "Good. I wanted to talk to you."

I was expecting a tongue-lashing, or at the very least, a good deal of ribbing.

"I just want to tell you how much I appreciate what you did out there tonight."

"What?" Were my ears playing tricks on me?

"You thought somebody was shooting at me, and you were trying to protect me. You were willing to cover my body with yours."

"I just didn't think about it. . . ."

"That's good, too, Dave. In a situation like that, if you take time to think about it, it might be too late. I just don't want you to feel bad about what happened out there tonight. You done okay." He socked me playfully on the arm.

I turned to go.

"Dave. . . ."

"Yeah?"

"You're a good brother, man. I love you."

I left Elvis's dressing room feeling like a giant. When Elvis had good things to say to you, everything was all right with the world!

*   *   *

When August came around, it was time for Elvis to get back to Las Vegas. But unfortunately for me, I wasn't going. The summer was almost over, so I was headed for Memphis and tenth grade at Hillcrest High School. I had never cared too much for school, but now it was unbearable.

My friend Jimmy Marberry felt about school the same way I did. It was wasting his time. He was ready to go to work full-time in his family's business.

"So what are we gonna do?"

"I don't know," Jimmy answered. It was lunchtime in the school cafeteria. The Salisbury steak didn't look all that appetizing. I wondered what Elvis was having for lunch.

"I can't take this anymore. I have to get back on the road with Elvis."

"What's stopping you? You're sixteen; you can quit school anytime you want to."

"Well, what about you? Why don't you just quit if it's that easy?"

"Because my parents would be on my back about it from here to doomsday—that's why not."

I pushed the tray away from me. "Yeah, mine too. I wish I could think of something that would make my mom think I was doing the right thing by dropping out."

I sat for a minute thinking, just watching Jimmy eat. Mom was the one I had to worry about. I knew Dad wouldn't object. After all, he would be on the road with me. Besides, I'd learned quite a bit about Dad on the last trip. He was no stick-in-the-mud when it came to knowing how to live it up on the road.

I had been home for only two days, and I was aching to get back on the road. That night, I told my parents that I just couldn't take school any longer, and I was going back on the road with Elvis. Once again, Mom gave me dozens of reasons why it would be a big mistake for me to leave school. With tears in her eyes, she begged me to reconsider. But it was no use. Mom was fighting a losing battle and she knew it. It was especially hard for her, because she felt that she'd already lost Rick. Rick had been touring with Elvis for two years and was becoming more and more entrenched in the world of show business. Mom had always wanted him to be a doctor, but that would never happen. And now, the same thing was happening to me.

There wasn't anything Mom could say to dissuade me. My mind was made up. That same night, I called Elvis, who was in an exuberant mood.

"David, buddy, what's up?" Before I could answer, he began telling me about Vegas. "Things are going great ... we're really packing 'em in! You ought to be here to pick up on some of this action!" That was all I needed to hear. I was through with school. I was heading back to Vegas. All I wanted to do from now on was rock 'n' roll!

On my first day back in Vegas, Elvis called me up to his suite. He had two heavily made-up Las Vegas show girls with him. "Welcome to Las Vegas, David. These two lovely ladies want to show you how much we've all missed you."

Ah, yes, this was definitely better than sitting in a geometry class.

The next day, Elvis told me he wanted me to start working closely with Red and Sonny. They were going to help turn me into a first-rate bodyguard. I was to start carrying a gun, and my karate training was to begin in earnest. Elvis had already been involved in karate for a few years, and he was quite good. I, too, knew something about the martial arts, but I had never taken serious training. Beginning immediately, I had instruction from the best—nationally known karate champions like Ed Parker, Bill Wallace, Dave Hepler, and

Tom Kelly. Elvis and I would work out together when he could make time, and he was delighted to see how much progress I was making.

A couple of times, I put a fancy move on him, thinking smugly that I would show him a thing or two. But he always paid me back. Almost before I knew what had happened, I would find myself sitting on the floor with a badly bruised ego.

The days in Vegas were all pretty much the same: Elvis would wake up about four or five in the afternoon and order his breakfast. He didn't want a whole bunch of people around, but usually Rick and myself, and perhaps one or two of the other guys, would be with him while he ate. We'd sit in his room and make small talk and watch television.

He loved to watch quiz shows, especially "The Match Game," which was always one of his favorites. "Hollywood Squares" was another game show Elvis liked, and we'd play along. If a football game was on, we'd watch that, or if he was flipping the channel selector and saw a Billy Graham crusade, he'd keep that on. Elvis didn't have a great deal of respect for TV evangelists in general, but he did like Billy Graham. Elvis had a very cynical nature, but he liked Graham's honesty and sincerity. I remember on one occasion, he was especially impressed when Dr. Graham preached a sermon on the kingship of Jesus Christ.

The following day, a fan called out to Elvis, "How ya doing, king?"

Elvis looked in the direction of the voice and pointed toward the sky. "Don't call me king," he said. "There's only one King!" Now, Elvis never set out to watch a Billy Graham broadcast. It's just that if one was on, he didn't turn the channel.

If there wasn't anything on television that Elvis wanted to watch, we'd just talk. We'd try to keep the conversation light, but it often turned to Lisa Marie and how much he loved and missed her, and to Priscilla and how she had hurt him. It worried me when Elvis got to talking about Priscilla, because he'd get angry, and I was always afraid it was going to affect his performance. But it didn't seem to, at least, not in 1972.

Around seven-thirty we'd leave the suite and head for the dressing room. It was time to get ready for the evening's first show. In the dressing room, Elvis would ask about the crowd and how things were going out there. He always seemed nervous, but once he got on that stage and the music started, all the nervousness disappeared. He had the audience in his pocket, and he knew it.

After the show, Elvis would go back to his room and rest up for the second show. The rest of us would go out to one of the other hotels in the area and have dinner, maybe gamble a little bit, and then come back in time to help Elvis get ready for the midnight show. By this time, most of the guys had picked out a girl to invite to the party after the show. The action didn't really get started until after that midnight show.

There were three tours that first year, and I learned quickly that life on the road was a mixture of pleasure and pain; and sometimes the pain could be intense.

Sometimes the pain came from Elvis's ardent fans. Elvis really knew how to work an audience, bringing everyone into a fever pitch with an up-tempo rock number, then cooling everything off with a dreamy ballad. But some of the fans didn't cool off very easily. I was punched, pushed, and kicked by fans who would do anything to get close to the man they adored!

I was smoking quite a bit of pot by then, but still trying to hide it from Elvis. I'll never forget how hurt he was the time he caught me. We were in Palm Springs, taking a short break between tour dates. He had gone out that day and bought himself a new black Sportster. Then he let me take it out for a ride.

I had always loved motorcycles, and I had a terrific time riding around on this one. When I got back to the house, I went up to Elvis's room to give the keys back. He was

Mom and my "new dad" on their wedding day, July 3, 1960.

My knee injury ended my football "career," much to Elvis's disappointment.

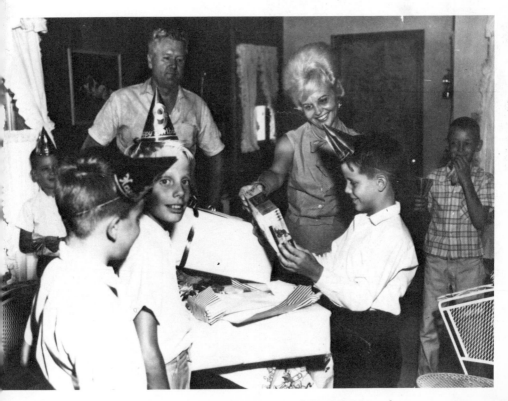

Mom, Dad, Billy, and Ricky helped me celebrate my ninth birthday in style.

When Priscilla Beaulieu came to live with us in 1962 it was like getting a new sister. The wedding, five years later, made it official. Priscilla, Mom, and Mrs. Kyle, a close family friend, celebrated at the wedding shower.

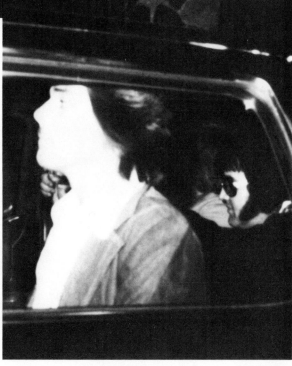

Finally being able to join Elvis full-time on his tours in 1972 made me feel like the "baddest dude" around. After all, how many 16-year-olds got to jet around the world with the king of rock 'n' roll?

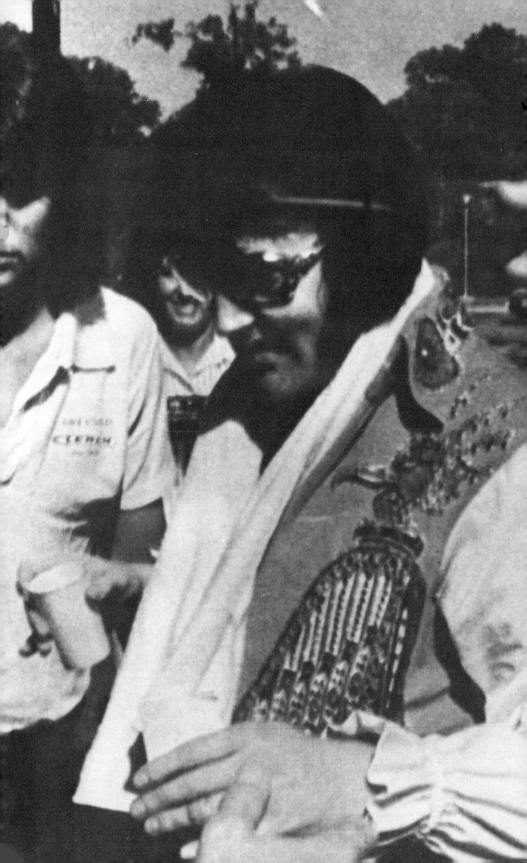

Left to right: Dick Grob, Joe Esposito, me, Elvis, and Ginger Alden.

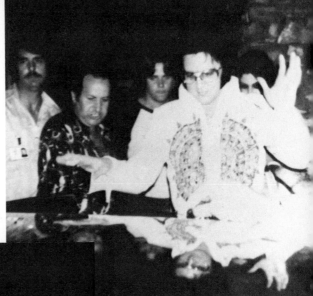

Dad was always popular with the fans, and he never missed a tour.

On my way to Las Vegas aboard Elvis's *Hound Dog One,* 1975.

Lamar Fike and I at Elvis's home on Hawaii's North Shore, 1972.

By 1977 the pressures of Elvis's life were evident in his appearance (top left).

Two days after Elvis's death, Mom, Rick, and I were still feeling the shock. It seemed like the whole world was mourning (above).

My brother Billy, our close friend Jackie Stovall, and I got together in Memphis in 1979.

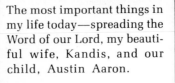

The most important things in my life today—spreading the Word of our Lord, my beautiful wife, Kandis, and our child, Austin Aaron.

around and stormed back up the stairs. Elvis was angry, but more than that, his feelings were really hurt. I flicked the joint away from me and looked up to heaven for help. I felt like dirt.

I went up to his room to apologize. He was just sitting there, sulking angrily.

"Elvis, I'm so sorry . . . but the tension has just been. . . ."

"Don't lay that tension crap on me!" He gave me that hard look of his that could just about burn holes through steel.

"Look, Elvis . . . I really am sorry. But at least I had enough guts to come up here and talk to you about it. I admit I was smoking dope, but at least I didn't take off running!"

He sat there for a minute, just looking at me. I felt as if I were on trial and awaiting the judge's decision.

Finally, he responded, "David, it's okay. Just don't let it happen again!"

Later on, he really lit into the other guys for running off.

That was another example of Elvis's double standard when it came to drugs. Marijuana was a recreational drug, and using dope for the fun of it was just plain wrong. Elvis took medicine because he felt he needed it, because he worked so hard. He figured a doctor would never give him something he didn't need. His little-boy trust in doctors got him in trouble in later years.

January found us in Honolulu, where he was getting ready to perform in his historical TV special, "Aloha From Hawaii." The show was being sent live, via satellite, to people all over the world. A conservative estimate was that more than one billion people would be watching and listening to Elvis perform.

As we waited backstage in the HFC Arena, he was more nervous than I had ever seen him before. He was shaking all over.

"David, I need you to do something for me. I can't find Dr. Nick."

He handed me a bottle full of some kind of liquid and a

hypodermic needle. He told me to stick the needle in the bottle and draw out some of the liquid.

I didn't know what was in the bottle, although I figured it was some sort of liquid vitamin; perhaps B_{12}.

When I finished drawing it out, he said, "Okay, now give me a shot."

I didn't move.

"David! I said, give me a shot!"

I just looked at him. "No."

Elvis's eyes opened wide. "No? What do you mean, no?"

"I'm just not going to do it!"

Elvis seemed furious, but he only asked me why I wouldn't give him the shot.

"Calm down," I pleaded. "You're fixing to go out on stage in front of a billion people."

"That's what this is for, to calm me down. You know how nervous I get before a big show, and this is no ordinary show."

At that point, another of Elvis's employees came over and took the needle from me. He gave me an exasperated look as he let out a heavy sigh: "Well, David, you'll learn."

He proceeded to give Elvis his shot.

Elvis snorted. "I love you for wanting to protect me, but when I want something done, *you had better do it!*"

After giving me those parting words, a pumped-up Elvis Presley went out and turned in a masterful performance.

*   *   *

In time, I did learn. I learned to do what Elvis wanted, and I learned that if someone made a threatening move, I acted quickly. There was no time to ask questions.

In New York City, we were leaving the hotel when I saw a man moving toward Elvis with something shiny in his hand. I grabbed him from behind by his hair and jammed my .38 halfway down his throat.

"One more step, and I'll blow your head off!"

The guy dropped the switchblade he was carrying, and the police quickly had him handcuffed and in custody.

Elvis hadn't even seen it happen. He was already in the limo yelling, "Come on! Let's go!"

When I finally got to the car, Elvis asked me what had taken me so long.

"I just saved your life," I answered. And then I told him what had just happened.

"Far out!" He patted me on the shoulder. "Well, that's what I pay you for, isn't it?"

Another time, in Ann Arbor, Michigan, we were all getting ready to board a bus, and out of the corner of my eye, I saw a guy coming up behind me. I turned around to see an angry-looking dude with brass knuckles and a taped right hand. I didn't give him a chance to do anything. I dropped him with a right to the jaw. And when he tried to get up, I decked him again.

Elvis was amazed at my quickness and my lack of fear.

Every tour, somebody would try to take a punch at Elvis, or threaten to shoot him. Jealous husbands would claim Elvis was flirting with their wives, and they'd be waiting for him in the hotel lobby; other guys just wanted to prove they were macho by beating up the king of rock 'n' roll.

Elvis told me that what he liked most of all about my work was that I reacted quickly, but I didn't overreact. Sonny and Red could be too rough, and they often mistook innocent actions for threats on Elvis's life. Several lawsuits had been filed, and Elvis was becoming more and more impatient with them. In their defense I should say that it was very easy to become trigger-happy because we were always on the lookout for danger.

Elvis could never understand why anyone would want to harm him. The very idea hurt him deeply. Sometimes he would get so upset about it that tears would roll down his cheeks. Years later, after an incident at the Silverdome in Pontiac, Michigan, he was especially upset.

"I don't understand, David, why would anyone want to kill me?" He was blinking back the tears.

I shrugged. I didn't have any answers.

"I've never done anything to hurt anyone. All I want to do is sing for people. Then some guy who doesn't even know me decides he wants to shoot me. Why?"

"There are just a lot of nuts out there, Elvis." It wasn't much comfort to him, but what else could I say?

In addition to the many real threats against Elvis's life, he was convinced that Mike Stone was going to send a hit man after him. Elvis had done a fair amount of threatening himself after Priscilla left him for Stone, but he was just blustering and bluffing. On January 8, 1973, Elvis's thirty-eighth birthday, and nearly eleven months after Priscilla walked out on him, Elvis filed for divorce. He was still not over the shock of her leaving, and never would be. But he had become convinced that reconciliation was impossible, and he wanted to get on with his life.

But it was not that easy.

In Las Vegas one time, during the middle of a concert, five men came out of the audience and tried to get on stage with Elvis. To this day, I don't know who they were or what they wanted. But Elvis was sure they were there to rough him up. As far as he was concerned, they were killers hired by Mike Stone.

Elvis took care of the first one with a disabling karate kick. Then Red and Sonny quickly dispatched the others. I didn't need to get involved, so I just sat on the sidelines and watched the whole thing. That was one wild evening!

Elvis had talked so much about getting even with Stone for stealing Priscilla, that he began to think Mike Stone was out to get him. Those fears were unfounded, but Elvis had reason for some of his worries. When Charles Manson was arrested for the Tate–LaBianca murders, it was revealed that he had an extensive hit list. Elvis Presley was one of the names on that list.

In 1974, when Patty Hearst was abducted by the Symbionese Liberation Army, there was talk that the radical group had targeted other famous people for kidnaping. Elvis was especially worried about Lisa Marie, who was staying with him at the time. When such stories hit the newspapers and television, those of us who were trusted with guarding Elvis's life were more jumpy, more ready to spring into action, and more likely to overreact.

We were in Lake Tahoe, Nevada, and, as usual, Elvis and his group had the entire top floor of the hotel. One night, the lights started blinking on and off. Then we heard a loud commotion; someone was banging on one of the exit doors at the end of the hallway.

Sonny and I went to check it out. I opened the door to see what was going on, and as I did, a man came through the door, pushing me to one side. He caught me off balance, and I fell back, but the guy hadn't bargained on Sonny. Sonny didn't wait to find out who the guy was or what he wanted; he just let him have it—knocked him to the floor. Then he jumped on top of the guy and held him down.

"I'm taking this guy back to my room. Go get Elvis."

Entering Elvis's room, I found myself looking down the barrels of two .45-caliber pistols! He was sitting on the bed, with both guns trained on the door, his daughter beside him. Anybody who tried to kidnap her wasn't going to be leaving alive. I was lucky he didn't shoot me.

I told him what had happened and that Sonny had taken the man into custody. Then we went to Sonny's room to try to talk to the guy and find out what he had been after.

When we got there, the man was handcuffed and lying on the bed, guarded by Red and Sonny. Elvis was really angry.

"You want to tell me what you mean by trying to break in here like that?"

The man didn't answer.

"Did you hear me? I want to know what you were doing. I'm not playing games with you."

Instead of answering, the man took a kick at Sonny. When Red saw that, he took a flying leap and landed on top of him, hitting him on the jaw with his fist. The man's head snapped back, and there was a sickening snap as his jaw was badly broken.

Blood began to pour out of his mouth, and the guy was obviously in a lot of pain. Elvis had never meant for that to happen, and he felt terrible. Even if the guy had been coming in to steal from us, Elvis hadn't wanted to hurt him.

"Red! What the . . . ? Mister, I'm sorry—I didn't want this to happen!"

We took the guy to another room, where we cleaned him up and Dr. Nick gave him emergency treatment. Then we sent him to a hospital for other repairs.

He wound up filing a $6-million suit against the Presley organization, claiming that he had been wrongfully injured. The case was eventually settled out of court, at a substantial cost.

For his part, Red couldn't understand why Elvis was so angry with him. Hadn't he just been doing his job? What was the big deal?

For Elvis, the incident was another reminder that Red and Sonny sometimes took things too far . . . that even though they were excellent bodyguards, their presence sometimes did more harm than good.

But then Elvis wasn't too sure about me either a couple of days later, when I almost shot Lisa!

We were still at Lake Tahoe, and Elvis was still afraid that the Symbionese Liberation Army might try to kidnap Lisa Marie. One night after the show, Elvis asked me to take Lisa back to the room, and keep her entertained for a while.

I had my .38-caliber pistol with me and decided that I would show her a thing or two about guns. We always left the first chamber empty. That way, it wouldn't be so easy in the heat of anger to just pull out your gun and start shooting. The first time you pulled the trigger, nothing would happen, and that gave you a second to think about what you were doing.

"Lisa," I said, "let me show you what I've learned about guns, sweetheart."

"I could take this gun and point it right at you and pull the trigger, and it wouldn't even hurt you."

"Really? Show me!" She stood at attention, sticking her chest out and holding her chin up. "Shoot me!"

"Well, one thing I've learned about guns is that you never, ever, point one at someone, even if you know it isn't loaded! But I'll show you what I'm talking about." I aimed at the chandelier and squeezed the trigger.

KAPOW! "Eeyow!" The gun went off, I yelled, bits of the chandelier went flying all over the room, and Lisa started bawling—all at the same time!

Elvis, Sonny, and the rest of the guys were just getting out of the elevator when they heard the gunfire. They came running, with their guns drawn.

"What is going on here?" Elvis demanded.

"That gun trick doesn't work!" was all I could say.

It goes without saying that Elvis wasn't happy with me. But I was finally able to convince him that I had been teaching Lisa the importance of never aiming a gun at anyone. That made him feel better, even if he was going to have to pay for the chandelier.

When we finally got her to quit crying and screaming, he had a little talk with her: "Now you listen to David, because he knows what he's talking about. He's a smart man."

Funny . . . I didn't feel very smart! I was still green behind the ears.

At least I had been smart enough not to point the gun at Lisa. It still makes me shiver when I think about what might have happened!

*   *   *

On tour, there was a tremendous amount of pressure on the entire group, and there was always the potential for disaster. As much fun as we had, it was always a relief to have a break.

103

Sometimes we would go to Colorado, where Elvis had a house in Vail. Elvis loved to snowmobile. He acted like a kid when it came to cold weather and snow.

One time while we were there, Elvis went out and bought cars for a couple of his friends on the Denver Police Department. That night the TV news had a piece about Elvis buying the cars. Following the story, the reporter threw in a personal note: "Hey Elvis! Are you out there? Listen, buddy, I sure would love a new Eldorado!" He went on to describe the car he wanted in detail. It was to be white with blue interior, automatic shift with cruise control, and so on.

When the guy finished, Elvis turned to me. "Did you get all that down?"

"I think so."

"Good. See if you can find a car just like the one he described. Have it delivered to him by tomorrow morning!"

I called several dealers until I found the right car.

The next night we watched the news again, to see if he would say anything about his new car. The first thing he said as he came on the air was, "Hey, Elvis, I was only kidding! But thanks! I'll keep the car!"

When we got back home to Memphis, my overzealousness landed me in trouble with Elvis again.

We had rented the Memphian Theater one night, and Elvis was with Linda Thompson. Linda was a former Miss Tennessee and a beautiful woman. She was also extremely bright, fun to be with, and definitely more than a short-time fling in Elvis's mind. At this point, she was also new on the scene, and Elvis was doing his best to impress her.

At the Memphian, Elvis usually sat in the center, about twelve rows from the front. His date sat by him, but nobody else sat in that row. It was understood that Elvis wanted the entire row to himself.

But a friend of Elvis's came in. He was a singer and songwriter, who had written several songs that Elvis had turned into hit records and had recorded several top hits of his own. But that night he had had a bit too much to drink and was in a very melancholy mood. He sat right behind Elvis and started talking loudly, "Elvis, you and I are a couple of lucky____, you know that? We're so____lucky!"

Elvis tried to hush him up, but he just kept it up. He was talking so loud you could hear him above the movie. And every other word out of his mouth was a swear word. Linda was a true Southern belle, a woman who didn't cuss, smoke, or drink, and Elvis knew this language wasn't impressing her at all!

Finally, Elvis got up to go to the rest room, and I followed him.

"Man, we've got to get rid of this guy," he said. "I just can't stand this!"

"I'll get rid of him."

"No, David, don't worry about it."

But I figured if Elvis wanted him gone, I'd get rid of him.

"I'll take care of it!"

So I went down and confronted him. "Listen, man, you're totally out of line here. You're a filthy toilet tongue, and I want you to leave!"

"Oh, yeah? Who do you think you are?"

I gave him my meanest look. "I told you, I want you to leave. Now don't make me throw you out!"

Just then, the guy saw Elvis returning from the rest room. And he did the last thing I expected him to do. He started crying.

"Elvis! You don't like me! I thought you were my friend, but you think you're too good for me. Who do you think you are?" and on and on. I couldn't get him to shut up, and Elvis was terribly embarrassed.

When we got home, Elvis jumped all over me. He was about as angry as I had ever seen him.

I said, "Well, you told me to get rid of him," but it wasn't any use. Elvis wasn't having any of that, and he lectured me for about fifteen minutes.

We saw the guy a couple of days later and he apologized for his behavior. It wasn't him talking that night—it was the Tennessee whiskey!

*   *   *

Those of us who worked for Elvis, whether we were on the road or at home, were always on duty, and the pressure could be tremendous. Sometimes I had to get away from it all, get out of town and away from the limelight. One time, Jimmy Marberry, Jackie Stovall, and I decided to drive to Florida. We were going to soak up some sun, drink ourselves silly, and check out the latest beach fashions.

When we got there, I decided that I would drop in on my real father, Bill Stanley. I knew he lived in Jacksonville and that he had remarried after my mom divorced him, but that was about all I knew. I hadn't seen him in over fifteen years. I didn't feel any anger toward him because he hadn't kept in touch. After all, he probably figured we were doing pretty well, since Mom had married into the family of Elvis Presley. But as I was getting older, I found myself wondering more about what kind of man he was.

When I called him and asked to see him, he sounded delighted. He and his wife, Lois, would love for us all to come. In fact, we could stay with them if we wanted to.

The first thing I found out about Bill Stanley was that he's a huge man, probably six foot eight and 270 pounds. When I first saw him at the door, I had the weirdest sensation, like I was shrinking! That's how big he is.

On that visit, I got a glimpse of the sort of man he is, and I learned to respect him. He told me that he had served as personal bodyguard for General Patton during World War II and that he had been part of Patton's Third Army that marched across Europe. He related story after story about the general, who was one of Elvis's favorite historical characters and so had become one of mine.

He didn't seem to mind talking about his war experiences, until I asked him how many enemies he had killed. When he tried to answer my question, he started crying. I told him he didn't have to talk about it if he didn't want to, but he said he wanted to tell me about it. He told me that as General Patton's personal bodyguard, he was ordered to shoot to kill any unauthorized person who came within a certain distance. He didn't know exactly how many men he had killed, but even one was too many.

He also wept as he remembered seeing his best friend killed by enemy fire. As he talked on, I began to realize why he had turned to the bottle for comfort.

Later on, I found out that Elvis was taking a swing through Florida and would be doing a couple of shows in Jacksonville. When I told my father about it, he was excited and said that he would come over and spend some time with us at our hotel. That was fine with me. It would be good to have a chance to introduce him to all the guys.

Dad kept telling me he wanted to talk to Elvis, so I went to Joe Esposito and asked him for a backstage pass. I planned to take him backstage to say hello to Elvis before the show that night.

So, right before the concert, Rick and I took our father backstage for a chat with Elvis. I kept my fingers crossed, and said a quick prayer, "Please don't let him say anything to make Elvis angry!"

Backstage, Elvis had just finished getting dressed. Dad looked at him and the first words out of his mouth were, "Well look what the cat dragged in!"

I looked at Rick. We were both thinking the same thing: *"There go our jobs!"*

But Elvis was cool. "Why, Mr. Stanley, nice to see you. How are you?" He extended his hand.

"Well, Elvis ... how are you?" and he whacked Elvis on the back, hard enough that Elvis staggered forward a step or two.

"Dad," I said, "it's almost time for the show to start. We're going to have to go."

We finally got him out the door, but by that time I was perspiring heavily. I could just picture Dad sticking his finger in Elvis's stomach and saying something like, "You're putting on a little weight, aren't you, fellow?" Thankfully, he didn't do that ... but I wondered how Elvis was going to react to his little "chat" with my father.

During the concert that night, several fans tried to rush the stage, as always happened when Elvis performed, and Dad jumped into the middle of the action, helping the security police: "Hold 'em back, boys!"

After the concert that night, we headed straight to the airport to fly out of Florida. We hadn't been in the air too long when Joe Esposito came and told Rick and me that Elvis wanted to talk to us. *Oh-oh.*

In my mind, I was already running over what to say. After all, it wasn't fair to blame me for what someone else might have said. Besides, the man was my father, and when he said he wanted to see Elvis, what else could I do?

But when Rick and I walked into Elvis's private compartment, Elvis seemed relaxed, and somewhat amused by it all. At least he didn't *look* angry!

"How you guys doing tonight?"

"Okay?" I said it more as a question than a statement.

"I want to ask you something.... You know what happened back there in the sixties ... are you two glad that happened?"

"Yeah," I said.

"Real glad!" Rick added.

"Just wanted to know." Elvis smiled.

Six

My Brother the Mystic

On the road with Elvis Presley, I was finding out more and more what a complicated individual he was. In many ways, Elvis was a walking contradiction. He was deeply spiritual, while at the same time living life in the fast lane.

One of Elvis's favorite books was the Bible. He carried it with him wherever he went. And in his billfold, he kept a picture of Jesus. If you were to walk into his room unannounced, you might find him reading the Bible or on his knees in prayer. But you would be just as likely to find him reading a book on numerology, or some other occult practice.

Elvis and I had many long talks during those days, and he would often want to talk about spiritual matters. I would sit at his feet like a young disciple and listen while he expounded on the nature of God.

I had learned from Vernon that Elvis had had an encounter with Jesus Christ when he was a young boy. The Presleys had been members of an Assemblies of God church in Tupelo, Mississippi, before they moved to Memphis, and Elvis had been saved in that church when he was nine or ten years old.

Vernon remembered how that experience had had a profound effect on Elvis, who was especially struck by Jesus' words to the rich young ruler: "Sell all that you have, and give the money to the poor" (see Matthew 19:21). Young Elvis had wanted to give all his toys away, including the only expensive thing he had, a brand-new bicycle.

I personally feel that during this time Elvis felt called to become a minister, a call he rejected when he became a star in the world of rock 'n' roll. And his rejection of that call caused him a great deal of dissatisfaction. No matter how rich he became, how many records he sold, how many adoring women threw their room keys at him, he knew he wasn't doing with his life all he was supposed to do. He never said as much to me, but he did tell me on more than one occasion that he should have become a preacher. I think he meant it.

For one thing, when Elvis sang gospel music, you could almost feel something supernatural happening. The only Grammy Awards he ever won came from his gospel albums. He meant the words he was singing, especially when he was recording his all-time favorite song, "How Great Thou Art."

Even during the seventies, he would sometimes hold Bible studies at Graceland or one of his other homes. It never seemed to dawn on him that his "students" were almost always young, beautiful women who didn't seem to be all that serious about their studies. He was trying to enrich their lives spiritually, and they had other things on their minds!

Elvis never lost interest in the realm of the spirit, but he began to believe the Bible needed further elaboration and explanation. That was a source of argument.

"David," he would tell me, "you can't just take the Bible at face value. It's too simple. You have to have something to explain it to you."

I hadn't been inside a church since I was fifteen, but I still believed the Bible was the inspired Word of God.

"Elvis, I just don't agree with that. In church we learned

that the Bible is God's Word, and whatever it says is true."

He found my simplistic approach amusing.

Looking back on it now, it's funny that we would spend so much time talking about religion in general and Christianity in particular, because neither one of us was living a very spiritual life. It is true, though, that every so often, Elvis would decide he needed purification, so he would abstain from sex, or medication, or what-have-you, and expected the same from us. Whenever that happened, we would roll our eyes toward heaven and silently pray that it wouldn't last too long. Elvis could be a real pain in the neck when he was in one of his super-spiritual moods!

What he really needed was a good Bible commentary. Instead, he began reading books that took an unorthodox view of Christianity, to say the very least. And then there was Larry Geller, Elvis's hairdresser, who had introduced him to a more mystical approach to religion. Elvis was caught up in the search for truth in an age when many young Americans were turning to Eastern religions, meditation, and the occult. He was no exception.

Two books that he especially enjoyed were *The Impersonal Life,* which talks a great deal about the subconscious, the God within, and so on, and *Cheiro's Book of Numbers* which is a guidebook to numerology.

The first time I saw him with that book, we were sitting around the pool at Graceland.

"David, when's your birthday?"

"August 30."

"Hmm. That makes you a three." He started flipping through the book. "This is interesting. You like bright colors, you're creative...." He kept going for a while, and almost everything he told me was accurate.

Some days later, he came to my room to talk to me, and as he looked around he nodded and said, "See ... I knew your room was going to look like this!"

Elvis's number was an eight, because he was born on January 8. So he tried to surround himself with eights. His color was emerald green, and so when he bought his own airplane, he had emerald green carpeting installed in it.

He never went so far as to let numerology control his life, but he would wear a certain color if it was the right day for it, or he would avoid people on a specific day if the number chemistry wasn't right.

Among all of Elvis's friends and acquaintances, I know of only one who tried to talk to him about his relationship with God, and that was Pat Boone. Elvis believed the Bible, just like I did, but the difference with Boone was that *he* lived out his belief. Elvis respected and admired Pat for that, but at the same time, that kind of approach to God was too simple for the king of rock 'n' roll.

I would often listen to Elvis talk about the supersubconscious, how the physical body is nothing but a shell for the spirit, and how someday we'll all be living in the light . . . at the time I took everything he said with a very large grain of salt!

Elvis's attitudes about life were shaped in part by his close association with death. His mother, Gladys, had died at forty-six, while Elvis was serving in the army, and on the eve of his scheduled departure for Germany. Her death affected him profoundly and probably prompted his search for the meaning of life—a search that took him far beyond the walls of orthodox Christianity.

Elvis also knew that his mother had carried twins when she had been pregnant with him. His brother, Jessie Garon Presley, had been stillborn. This was another brush with eternity that Elvis felt deeply.

But I don't believe that Elvis was obsessed with either the death of his mother or of his twin brother. It's just that these two incidents planted seeds in his mind that helped develop his mystical outlook on life. Some people have painted a picture of Elvis as a mama's boy who never got over his mother's death, but I don't think that was true. Elvis and I had many long talks during those days on the road, and he never talked to me about his mother or how much he missed her. It's true that he never referred to my mother as "Mom," but then he was already twenty-five years old when she married Vernon Presley.

Elvis loved his mother and there's no doubt that her death hurt him deeply. After all, he was her only child, and the Presleys had always been a very close family. But Elvis did not spend the rest of his life grieving.

The stories about Elvis's relationship with his mother probably got started for two reasons: First, because he bought a home for his parents when he first became a star. In those days, everything Elvis did was done in the glare of the spotlight. So he immediately became known as a fine boy who loved his mother. (And remember that Elvis was just twenty years old when "Heartbreak Hotel" spent eight weeks at the top of the record charts.)

The second reason for those stories was that Elvis was obviously distraught at his mother's funeral and made no attempt to hide his pain and his tears. But who wouldn't cry at his mother's funeral?

From those incidents, an entire legend sprang up about his obsession with his mother and his perpetual mourning and grieving over her death.

I don't know how the stories about Elvis and his twin brother got started. I've seen the reports that Elvis always felt he was living for both himself and Jessie Garon. I've read that he often carried on conversations with his twin and that he often felt as though his twin were with him. My reaction is that such stories are pure nonsense, the stuff from which legends are constructed—the sort of legends that are bound to grow up around someone as popular as Elvis Presley.

Elvis did not live his life in bondage to people who had died years before. I'm sure he thought about his mother, and perhaps about his brother, too, but not in an obsessive, sick sort of way.

Another time Elvis was touched by death was when a girl he was fond of was killed in an automobile accident. Just the day before her death, she and Elvis had gone out on a date and had been photographed sitting astride one of his motor-cycles. She was a pretty girl, full of life, and in that photo-graph she had a big smile on her face. They had talked and laughed and had a good time together ... and the next day she was killed.

Elvis didn't know the girl all that well. In fact, she was someone he thought he would like to get to know better, but now he would never get the chance. Upon hearing of her death, Elvis retreated to his favorite place for reflection, Meditation Gardens. He asked me to come and sit with him.

We sat again, looking at the statue of Jesus and then at some silvery clouds that floated across the full moon.

"You know, David, it was really a tragedy that she had to die—especially the way she did."

I nodded my agreement.

"But when you come out here where you can think, and your mind is clear, you realize that death isn't the end. Really, it's only the beginning." He bent down and picked up a pebble, which he held in the palm of his hand.

"The human body isn't really anything but a lump of clay, just like this old rock. When her body was all tangled up in that twisted metal, that wasn't really her. She'd already gone on ... to another existence ... elsewhere."

He tossed the rock away, and it landed a few feet in front of us. "The body is just the shell that contains the spirit."

We heard a siren race past on Elvis Presley Boulevard, an ambulance on its way to an emergency call.

"This life is so uncertain. What about you, David, are you afraid of dying?"

I hadn't thought about it very much. After I thought for a minute I said, "No. I don't fear death, but I do fear God."

"Well, you're very wise to fear God. So do I ... so do I." Then we sat in silence, each lost in our own thoughts.

I mentioned before that Elvis sometimes wondered why he was so popular. All you had to do was see him in concert to realize that he had an uncanny power over people. That wasn't something he learned—it had always been there. Elvis Presley wasn't the only man doing rock 'n' roll during the fifties, but he had that extra dimension that made him the immediate favorite. He always knew that his popularity was a gift from God, but he was never sure what to do with it, or why he'd been the one chosen for it.

He came to believe, and not in a boasting or prideful way, that he must be a very special person in God's sight. Whenever he thought about it, he felt very humbled and always reacted with a "why me?" attitude.

Eventually, he felt that he had been given other special abilities.

One humid summer afternoon we were lazing around in the pool at Graceland. I was floating around in the deep end of the pool, while Elvis was lying out in the sun, working on his tan. Suddenly the sun disappeared behind a large black cloud.

"Hey, David," Elvis called to me. "You want to see something?"

"Sure."

"Watch this." He stood up and held his hand out in the direction of the sun. His hand was shaking as he brought it slowly from left to right across the cloud.

"What are you doing?"

"Shhhh!" He repeated the motion a few more times until the cloud had finally moved away.

"There you go!" He smiled triumphantly. "I moved that cloud away from the sun. Pretty good, huh?"

He shot me a look out of the corner of his eye to see whether I believed him or not. It was sometimes hard to tell when he was serious and when he was just teasing. But that time, he convinced me that he had caused the cloud to move across the sky.

Not long after that, when several of us were driving across the desert from Las Vegas to Palm Springs in Elvis's Trans Am, one of those violent desert thunderstorms blew up. We were driving under bright sunshine, but directly ahead of us the sky was a deep, threatening purple. Every few seconds the entire sky would be lit up by a brilliant flash of lightning.

One of the guys said, "Boy . . . looks like we're really in for it!"

Elvis, who was driving, said, "Nah . . . I'll take care of it."

"What do you mean by that?" I asked.

"Just watch."

As we entered the storm, Elvis stuck his right hand out through the sunroof and started talking to the clouds. "I order you to let us pass through! I order you to move to the side and leave us alone!"

And the amazing thing was that the clouds did exactly as he asked them to! They split right down the middle. It was coming down in buckets to our left and our right, but we drove right through the storm without getting so much as one drop on our windshield.

Elvis pulled his hand back into the car. "See."

The rest of us all began to look at one another. "Is this really happening?"

I thought the whole thing was just a coincidence, but I certainly wasn't going to try to tell that to Elvis.

Elvis also believed he had the ability to heal people through the laying on of hands, and I have to say that in certain instances, he did.

More than once, I had headaches so bad I felt as though my head were about to explode.

Elvis would lay his hands on my head and speak to me in a soothing voice: "Just relax, David. The headache is going away. Your head feels fine." And sure enough, in a matter of minutes, the headache would be completely gone.

Once, we were skiing in Colorado, and Dean Nichopoulos, who was one of Elvis's aides, fell and twisted his leg badly. He was writhing around in the snow, screaming in pain. I was afraid his leg was broken, and I knew we were going to have to call for a stretcher to get him off the slopes.

But Elvis came over, bent down, and put both his hands on Dean's leg. He sat there for a second with his eyes closed, concentrating. Suddenly, Dean sat up, looking very surprised. "Hey! It doesn't hurt anymore!"

He was able to get up and walk back to the lodge.

How was Elvis able to do things like that? That's something that, to this day, I find myself wondering about. I know he knew exactly what to do and what to say to get people to relax and get their minds off their problems. But I also believe that Elvis had some God-given abilities that the average person doesn't have.

Elvis chose to be a rock 'n' roll star. But if he had chosen to be a preacher, there's no telling what other great things he might have done!

Seven

An Angry Young Man

"Hey David, I'm thirsty ... run out and get me a Coke."

"Yeah. Me, too. And while you're at it, bring me a newspaper."

"Dr. Pepper for me."

We were sitting around in Elvis's suite at the International Hotel, and, as usual, some of the guys were trying to order me around. Because I was the youngest member of the group, the guys sometimes got the idea that I was there merely to wait on them, but I wasn't having any of it.

I kept looking at my magazine and mumbled an obscenity under my breath.

"What did you say?" Red West grabbed the magazine out of my hands.

"I said you guys can drop dead! And give me back my magazine!" I made a grab for it, but Red tossed it over to Dick Grob.

"Listen, punk! Don't you dare talk to me that way."

"Oh, yeah? Why don't you stick it where you can't see it? Nobody's gonna tell *me* what to do!"

"You little brat!"

Red stepped through the door into Elvis's dressing room. He motioned for me to join him.

"Get your butt in here! Let's find out how tough you are."

That was fine with me. I wasn't afraid of Red West—or anybody else.

When I walked into the room, he shut the door behind me. Then he put his face right up next to mine. His voice was shaking with anger: "Don't you ever talk to me that way again. If you do, I'll tear your head off!"

I pushed him away from me. "Why don't you shut your stupid mouth and leave me alone!"

The next thing I knew I was bouncing off the wall. He hit me so hard, I thought I saw some of Elvis's angels!

I lay on the floor rubbing my painful jaw, while Red stood over me, ready to knock me down again if I tried to get up.

"That's just a taste of what you're going to get if you don't keep your mouth shut and do what you're told." Then he stormed out of the room, shutting the door behind him.

I just walked out of the dressing room and headed for my room. When I got there, the phone was ringing. It was Red.

"Listen, David, that was just a misunderstanding in there. That's all. Okay?"

I rubbed my sore jaw. I was still so angry, I didn't want to talk about it.

Later on, the phone rang again. This time it was Elvis. He wanted to see me. Elvis never did like to talk over the phone. If he had something to say to you, he wanted to say it in person, to your face. So I went to his suite.

"I heard you had a bit of a problem today. Want to tell me about it?"

I shrugged. "I smarted off to Red, and he dropped me."

"That's it?"

"That's it."

I explained to Elvis that I had thought I was going to kill Red. "And if he ever hits me again, I *will* kill him!" Then I explained how the guys had been ordering me around, treating me as if I were their slave.

"Well, David, you're working for me and not for anyone else. You don't take any orders from anyone."

I turned to go.

"But David." I stopped with my hand on the doorknob. "Try to control your temper."

I gave him the thumbs-up sign as I walked out the door.

That wasn't going to be easy for me to do. My job as a bodyguard required me to be on my toes at all times. I had to be ready to fight, ready to go for my gun. It wasn't easy to be a tough guy when on duty and a nice guy the rest of the time.

Another problem for me was that I simply got tired of looking at the same old faces. When we were on tour, we were like a large family, with way too much family togetherness. It seemed like we were together all the time, and the pressures on each of us were phenomenal. In a situation like that, arguments and fights were bound to break out, especially when the tension was further inflamed by booze and drugs. And some of us were using both heavily.

Elvis himself added to the tense atmosphere by his extreme moodiness. Whenever he wanted something, no matter what time it was, he expected us to be ready to get it for him. On the other hand, sometimes he would spend weeks at a time locked in his room, barely communicating with the rest of us. But we had to be there waiting, just in case. The waiting was the worst part, because the monotony was nerve-racking. It was like being in an Ingmar Bergman movie, sitting around listening to the clock tick the hours away.

*   *   *

In 1974, I married a girl named Angie. While I was on the road, she was waiting at home in Memphis. That was something that weighed heavily on my mind, being away from her so much. Angie didn't care too much for it either, especially because she knew that my first loyalty was always to Elvis, not to her. Whenever he needed me, I'd go running. I truly loved Angie, but like many of the other guys, when we were out on the road, I thought nothing about trying to score with any attractive woman who came along.

As soon as I was on the airplane, my wedding ring came off my finger and my little black book came out. That's the way the people I looked up to did it, and that's the way I did it, too.

There's no excuse for behaving that way, but, in my defense, I had extremely poor role models. I knew that when Elvis was married to Priscilla he had girl friends on every tour. And on my first tour, I saw my own stepfather in the company of attractive women. That was just the way life was. I never thought about Elvis's behavior hurting Priscilla; I never thought about Dad fooling around on Mom; and I never gave a second thought to the fact that I was being unfair to Angie.

During the summer of 1974, I was on my second tour following my marriage to Angie. We were in Philadelphia. Several of us were sitting around in the hotel, having a few drinks, and generally unwinding from a day's work. There was a girl there that one of the guys was interested in, but I thought he was treating her like dirt. I didn't know if he had had too much to drink, or exactly what his problem was, but he was really lecturing her.

"You're here with me . . . you understand that? And I don't want you talking to anybody else . . ." and on and on.

Finally, I'd had enough of it. I wasn't interested in the guy's girl friend, but I felt sorry for her.

"Look, man," I said, "you don't own her!" Then I turned to her. "Don't listen to him. He can't tell you what to do."

"I think I'd just like to leave," she said.

I told her if she wanted to leave, she should feel free to go. And just to make sure she wasn't hassled anymore, I'd walk her to the elevator.

She gave me her hand, and we headed for the door. Her boyfriend didn't try to stop us; he just stood there glaring at me. Just as we left the room, I heard him yell, "You____, I'll show you!"

I stuck my head back in the door and gave him my most disdainful look. "Hey, man, don't be such a jerk!"

As we walked to the elevator, the girl suggested that perhaps she and I could go somewhere together—just the two of us. But I told her I wasn't interested, that I was only trying to help her get away from her friend. I realized, though, that if she thought I was interested in her, he thought so, too. And he wasn't going to let me get away with it.

After she left, as I was about to reenter the room, I heard the guy over in the corner talking to Rick. Rick was trying to quiet him down, but he was agitated and talking loudly. "When we get home, I'll fix him. I'm going to tell Angie that he's been chasing every girl he sees!"

I was standing in the doorway. "Hey, jerk! You want to repeat what you just said?"

He turned and pointed at me. "I said, when we get home I'm going to tell Angie about all the chicks you've been sleeping with."

I walked toward him, picking up a heavy glass ashtray from the nearest table. "Don't you ever say anything like that again!"

"I'm not only going to tell her about them. I'm going to give her names and phone numbers . . . that way if she doesn't believe me she can call them and find out for herself!"

That did it! I threw the ashtray as hard as I could and hit him squarely in the chest.

"Ow!" He grabbed his chest and doubled over. Then he straightened up and came running toward me. "Why you—"

Before he could touch me, I reached out with a sidekick and knocked him up against the wall.

Rick jumped in front of me. "No, David, don't! He's drunk!"

I grabbed Rick's shoulders and threw him up against the

wall; then I was on top of the other guy. I was totally out of control. I hit him again and again and again! His eyes were swollen and his lips were bleeding, and still I kept on punching. I didn't seem to be able to stop myself. It was like all the anger and frustrations I had ever felt were pouring out of me, and this poor guy was feeling the brunt of them.

Red came up behind me and tried to pull me off. I turned around and took a swing at him. Then I was back on top of my opponent. Dick Grob grabbed me, and I started swinging at him, too.

Then I heard Dad's voice. "David!" When I heard him it was like I returned to reality. I just stopped and looked down at the guy lying unconscious on the floor. I couldn't believe what I had done.

Hotel security had arrived by this time, and they hand-cuffed me. Then they brought in someone to take my victim to the emergency room. He looked half-dead, and I hated myself for what I had done.

After they took a statement from me, the hotel security let me go back to my room. Rick came with me, and we just sat there looking at each other.

"What in the world did I do?" I asked him. "I almost killed him! I can't believe it."

I decided that I'd better tell Elvis about it before somebody else did. It was my job to wake him up every day and get his breakfast, so I'd tell him first thing the next day; I might as well get it over with. There was no doubt in my mind that my days as one of Elvis's bodyguards were over.

The next day, I went in and woke him up. We made small talk for a while, and then I turned on "The Match Game" while he was eating. Finally, I screwed up my courage.

"Elvis, there's something I have to tell you."

"What?" He was still paying more attention to the television than he was to me.

"Listen, Elvis, I did something that's going to make you mad. I'm sure you're going to kick my rump, and you're probably going to fire me."

That got his attention. "What in the world did you do?"

I swallowed. "I beat the hell out of one of the guys last night."

"You did *what?*"

At that exact moment, the guy walked into the room. He looked as if he'd been beaten with a baseball bat. His eyes were swollen to the point of being almost shut, his lips were swollen and blue, and he had stitches in his chin and under his left eye.

Elvis stopped eating, and his mouth dropped open. Then he turned to me. "My God, David, what did you do?"

Before I could answer, the guy walked up and hugged me. I hugged him back, uncertainly. I was afraid he had a knife and was going to stab me in the back.

He looked at Elvis. "I just said the wrong thing."

I tried to tell Elvis what had happened, and the other guy backed me up all the way. But Elvis just kept looking at his face. This was one of his closest friends, looking like he'd taken a trip through a meat grinder.

As soon as he'd left the room, Elvis was all over me.

"How in the world could you beat up one of my best friends? How could you hurt him like that?"

I looked down at the floor, not knowing what to say.

"You can just get out of my sight! I don't ever want to see you again. I don't want to have to look at your face."

"But Elvis, I...."

"I said get out of here and I meant it." He pointed at the door.

I knew better than to stand there and argue with him, so I left. The next day, I went back to talk to him again, but his attitude hadn't changed.

"What are you doing here?" he demanded. "Didn't I tell you I didn't want to see you? Now get out of here!"

Elvis didn't talk to me for several days, and I was miserable, just hanging around not knowing what to do. Most of the other guys were keeping their distance, too. They had been shocked by the violence of my outburst. Even Red and

Sonny, who were not noted as peace-lovers, were surprised by the beating I'd given that guy.

Finally, on the fourth day after Elvis had told me to get out of his sight, I decided to make another attempt. I went to his dressing room as he was getting ready for that evening's show.

When I walked in, he looked up and gave me an exasperated look, as if to say, "What do you want now?" But before he could say anything I jumped in.

"Look, Elvis. You've been yelling at me and jumping all over me for beating up your friend, and I'm really sorry about that. But I want to ask you a question."

He looked at me for a moment, and then said, "Go ahead." At least he was willing to listen.

"What would you have done if you had been in my place? What if someone had come to you a couple of years ago and said, 'I'm going to tell Priscilla that you're sleeping with every chick in the country'?"

He shrugged. "I . . . uh. . . ."

"Elvis! You would have killed him!"

He thought for a minute and then said, "You're right. I would have killed him. But just be cool. He didn't really do it. He was only running his big mouth."

"Well?"

"Okay, David, I see your point. But look, man . . . try to stay mellow. Don't go around beating up on the staff."

"Okay," I agreed. "But that jerk had just better watch what he says from now on. No telling what I might do next time."

That next time almost came on the eve of our next tour. We were at Graceland, early in 1975, preparing to head out on the road for several weeks.

Angie and I were sitting in the living room, and I was telling her how much I was going to miss her and how I hated to go.

Then that same guy came walking through the house.

"All right! Tour time! Chicks . . . drugs . . . sex!" He looked over at me and winked. "Better get out your little black book, David! It's tour time!" Then he walked on into the den.

I felt like going after him right then, but I remembered what had happened before, and I didn't want a repeat of that.

Angie looked at me and started crying. Tears were rolling out of her big eyes, and I could feel my heart sinking.

"Don't listen to him," I told her. "He's just trying to be a big shot. He's just teasing!"

Angie didn't like me going on tour all the time anyway. She wanted me to stay home, get a nine-to-five job, and be a typical husband. It was hard for her when I was gone, and these comments certainly weren't going to make her feel better about things.

As soon as I could, I excused myself and went upstairs to look for Elvis. He was in his bedroom, getting together a few books he wanted to take with him on the tour.

"Elvis, I need to talk to you for a second."

"Sure. What's on your mind?" He motioned me over to the nearest chair.

"What I want to tell you is ... that there's a little jerk downstairs, and if he doesn't shut his mouth, I'm going to kill him!"

Elvis gave me a puzzled look, so I went on to tell him what his friend had been saying and how he had upset Angie.

Elvis immediately got on the phone and called downstairs. "I need to see you. Will you come upstairs right now?"

A few minutes later, the guy came bouncing into the room, smiling and laughing. He was anxious to get back out on the road, and he was really wound up.

"What's this I hear about you shooting off your mouth downstairs?"

The smile disappeared. He shrugged. "Well, I didn't mean to—"

"Don't you remember what happened last time you started talking like that?" Elvis interrupted.

His pal didn't answer; he just turned and looked at me.

"I've told David to keep his temper under control," Elvis went on, "but if you don't keep your mouth shut, I'm not going to be responsible for anything he does."

"Okay. I didn't mean to cause any trouble."

"Just be careful what you say and who you say it to."

"Okay. David," he stuck out his hand, "I'm sorry if I caused a problem."

I took his hand and we shook. "It's all right . . . I just had to do some fast explaining."

From then on, he was pretty good to watch what he said around me, at least as far as Angie was concerned. As for me, I tried to keep my marriage together by bringing her along on the next tour. It was not easy trying to do my job while at the same time keeping her from finding out what usually went on when we were on the road. I lived in fear that one of the guys would say or do something to give me away. I nearly panicked once or twice when I saw a woman I had become acquainted with on a previous tour. What would I do if she said something in front of Angie? "David! Glad you're back in town. Will I see you tonight?" That would have been the end of my marriage, no doubt about it.

But the tour passed without incident, and we all headed for Elvis's house in Palm Springs for a few days of relaxation. By the time we got there, I was being my usual belligerent self, and Angie was probably wishing she had stayed home.

One day, I was particularly angry with her for some reason and I was yelling at her. I don't remember what she had done, but it was taking less and less to light my fuse those days. Whatever it was, I was really angry.

Another member of the Memphis Mafia, who at this time weighed around 320 pounds, was sitting in the living room with us, and he decided I was getting out of hand.

"Lighten up, David!"

"This is none of your business! This is between me and my wife."

Angie got up from the sofa and started to run out of the

room. I grabbed her arm, but she got away from me and went running into the kitchen.

"Angie," I screamed, "come back here!"

"That's enough!" The guy made it sound like a threat.

"I told you to shut up, fat boy!"

He stood up and moved toward me. "One more word and I'll drop you right here!"

Ignoring him, I headed for the kitchen and Angie. But he stepped in front of me, blocking my path.

Whack! I hit him right across the side of his face. His glasses shattered and pieces went flying everywhere. He put his hands over his eyes, trying to protect himself from the flying glass. I walked around him and went into the kitchen for Angie. Then she and I went outside, where we finished our "conversation."

Naturally, when Elvis found out what had happened, he was livid.

"What in the world are you trying to do—kill all my friends?"

He paced back and forth in front of me, talking *at* me more than to me. "I don't know what I'm going to do with you! Your temper is going to get you in big, big trouble one of these days. I've told you over and over to keep it under control, and it just seems like you can't do it! What is wrong with you?"

"Elvis, it's the pressure. Sometimes I think I just can't take it anymore!"

I didn't tell him that it was also the drugs. I was taking them in ever-increasing amounts, and they were becoming a real problem for me. I was also upset by Elvis's life-style. His doctors were prescribing larger and larger doses of his medication, and I was worried about him. He was spending more time in his room, alone, cut off from everyone else. And he needed more medication to get him to sleep, and more to wake him up.

Sometimes I thought all the crap I was taking would end up killing me. I also thought all the medication the doctors were giving Elvis would end up killing him, too. He let them give him anything they wanted. He had total trust in professional people. He figured they knew best.

Finally, Elvis decided to give me a few weeks off. He wanted me to go to Seattle, where I would stay with a friend, under orders to "mellow out."

*   *   *

Another thing causing me a great deal of pain during late 1974 and 1975 was that my parents had decided to get a divorce.

I knew that Vernon had been seeing a lot of a young woman named Sandi Miller. He came to me one day on tour and asked me what I thought of her.

"I think she's a neat lady."

"Well, son— " he had a sheepish look on his face— "I'd like to talk to you about something."

"I don't want to talk about it, Dad. It's okay."

I know it sounds funny, that a man would seek to have his son's approval for an extramarital affair, but that's how twisted life had become for those of us who lived our lives in the fast lane.

Rick and I could both see that Dad was happy when Sandi was around, and if that's what he wanted, it was fine with us.

Mom knew something was going on. She would ask me from time to time what was happening on the road, and I'd tell her that I didn't know anything.

Sometimes she'd call me when we were on the road and tell me how lonely she was and how much she missed me. She would also say that she was praying for me, asking the Lord to watch over me and protect me. I appreciated her prayers and told her that. And I was sorry that she was lonely, but my job was to be on the road with Elvis.

I knew she was going through a rough time, that things

were not so good between her and Dad. I also knew that she was afraid she had lost her sons and her husband. And, in reality, she had. I felt sorry for her, but nobody told me what to do or how to live my life except Elvis. And when I did what Elvis wanted me to do, he paid me for it.

I felt that Dad's relationship with Sandi Miller was his business, not mine.

Finally, though, Mom found out what was going on between Dad and Sandi, and she filed for divorce. Their marriage went the way of most of the marriages around Elvis Presley and his fast-paced world of rock 'n' roll. With Mom and Dad getting a divorce, another wedge had been driven into our family, and I had lost my last link with a normal, healthy life-style.

When we found out that our parents were getting divorced, Elvis asked me how I felt about it.

"I hate it," I told him.

"So do I. I didn't want this to happen to them. I just want you to know, David, that I love you guys. As far as I'm concerned, you'll always be part of my family."

Then he asked the question that was uppermost on his mind.

"Do you have any problem with staying on with me?"

"Are you kidding? Whatever's happening between them—that's their problem. That doesn't have anything to do with us."

"Good. I was hoping you'd feel that way."

*   *   *

My time in Seattle was terrific. I didn't listen to rock 'n' roll, I didn't think about rock 'n' roll, and I tried to pretend I had never even heard of Elvis Presley. The one thing I didn't give up, though, were my drugs. Hey—I needed them!

When I got back on the road, I was feeling pretty good. I was even able to laugh at Elvis's jokes and get along with the rest of the guys. But then Elvis went into one of his moods again, and my newfound "mellow" nature disappeared quicker than a snowfall on the desert.

We were in Las Vegas, and Elvis had shut himself away from the rest of us. It was one of those times when we were waiting around for him to decide to do something—anything. Finally, he called me to his room.

Elvis had a doctor friend in Las Vegas. When he couldn't get his medication from Dr. Nick for some reason, he'd call his friend.

I got the doctor on the phone. "Elvis asked me to call you. He needs a few things."

To my surprise, the doctor said no. "Elvis doesn't need anything. He just thinks he does!"

I went back to Elvis, who was lying in bed watching TV.

"I'm sorry, but the doctor says he won't give you anything."

He jumped out of bed. "He says what? Get him back on the phone and tell him I feel terrible!" He started yelling, "You don't ask him anything . . . you tell him. I want relief now!"

I went back and called the doctor again.

"This is David again. Elvis is really freaking out . . . he told me to call you back and—"

"Look, I'm sorry if he's giving you a bad time. But I already told you—he doesn't need anything!" There was a loud click as he banged the phone down on its receiver. He meant business.

Elvis was still back in the bedroom of his suite; most of the other guys were sitting around in the sitting room watching TV or playing cards. A few of them rolled their eyes to let me know they understood what I was up against.

I went back to Elvis. "Hey, I'm really sorry, but the doctor still says no. Why don't you just forget it for a while?"

"Forget it? What are you talking about? I'm not going to forget it!"

"Hey, just cool off a little bit, man. I'm going downstairs to gamble for a while."

He stuck his finger right in my face. "You're not going any-where!"

"Come on, man! Just cool your jets, okay?"

He pushed his pajama sleeve up and took another step to-ward me. "Did you hear what I said?"

"Well, don't worry about it, okay? Man, you're driving me crazy! I have to go for a walk." And I turned away and walked out of his room.

Elvis came running out the door behind me. He had a .45 in each hand, and he was pointing them at my back.

"Stop! You____!"

I turned around. He was absolutely beside himself with rage. He jumped up on a table, while everybody else scram-bled for cover. We all thought he was going to start blasting away.

Instead, he looked at me. "Anybody who doesn't like it here can just get the hell out!"

Having said that, he jumped down off the table, strode back into his bedroom, and slammed the door.

I looked around at the guys. I slammed my fist down on the nearest end table; the glass shattered.

"I don't have to take this," I said. "I'm sick of this! You guys tell Elvis he can shove it!" And I walked out the door.

I got a cab to the airport and caught the next plane to Nashville. Angie was staying in an apartment there, because her parents lived there and that was where she wanted us to settle down. All during the trip home I kept thinking of how wrong Elvis had been to abuse me like that. I started think-ing that I had really done the right thing. The more I thought about it, the better I felt. I was going to do what Angie had always wanted me to do!

When I called Angie from the airport in Nashville, she was surprised and delighted to hear my voice. I had left Las Vegas in such a hurry, I hadn't even called to let her know I was coming.

She picked me up at the airport, and all the way home I gave her promise after promise. I was going to stay this time. I'd had enough of being on the road all the time. I was going to get myself a regular nine-to-five job, and we'd settle down in Nashville. Maybe it was time for us to start thinking about children.

She was so happy she could hardly contain herself.

"Praise God!" she said. "This is great!"

But after we had been sitting around the apartment for a while, I started feeling bad about what I had done.

I popped open a beer and sat sipping it while thinking about all the good times on the road. Elvis hadn't meant to yell at me, I reasoned. Life on the road was hard on me, but wasn't it even harder on him?

Maybe I ought to at least call and see if he had calmed down any. Sure, why not?

When I called, Elvis's cousin Billy Smith answered the phone.

"Hey, Billy," I tried to sound upbeat, "I'm just calling to see if Elvis has come down yet."

"No . . . not really."

"Well, what's going on there now?"

"He told us to get ready, because we're heading back home tomorrow."

That night, I didn't sleep well. All the way home I had been completely sure I was doing the right thing. And now that I was home, I was becoming just as sure that I had acted rashly and unwisely.

The next day, I called Graceland; Billy Smith answered again.

"Billy, it's David. Is Elvis all right?"

"Yeah, David, he's fine. He's been asking about you. He really wants you to come back."

As soon as I heard those words, I knew that was what I was going to do. I asked Billy if I could talk to him.

"Yeah, let me see if he's able to talk to you."

In a few minutes, Elvis came on the line.

"Hey buddy, how you doin'?"

"Well . . . I'm kind of feeling bad."

"Me, too. Listen, I'm sorry about what happened. I didn't mean to, uh. . . ."

"Yeah, I know. Me neither. I'm sorry, too. But I've got to tell you, Elvis, sometimes I think those doctors are killing you with all that medication. I don't think you need it as much as you think you do."

"But I only take what I need!" There was that self-justifying attitude again.

"All I know is that sometimes I can hardly stand to be around you. I worry about you, you know."

I didn't know how he'd take that and was relieved when he chuckled.

"David, why don't you get your butt back over here?"

"Yes, sir!"

"And David . . . don't ever leave me again. I need you, man!"

"I won't. You can count on me."

When I told Angie that I was going back to work for Elvis, she was crushed.

"What about all those promises you made?"

I shrugged. "He needs me."

"He needs you? What about me? Don't you think I need you?"

"Angie . . . try to understand. . . ."

"I've been trying to understand ever since we've been married. Only it's getting harder and harder!"

I didn't know what else to say. I'd made up my mind, and that was all there was to it. But what I didn't understand was that my decision to go back to work for Elvis was also a decision that had cost me my marriage.

I wasn't walking back into any fairy-tale "happily-ever-after" with Elvis either. It wasn't too long before I was back in trouble. Elvis was angry with me for some reason, and I was off the payroll for three months. During this time, Rick also lost his job.

Rick was laid off when Elvis found out he had been bad-mouthing Elvis's girl friend, Linda Thompson.

"That Linda Thompson really thinks she's hot stuff. Well, she's not so great," and on and on. What Rick didn't know was that Linda was standing at the top of the stairs and heard every word he said. Her feelings were hurt, naturally, and she told Elvis. Elvis was very close to Linda at that time, and he had to prove his loyalty to her. So Rick found himself standing in the unemployment line with me.

I soon found a job pumping gas into private airplanes at the High Air Airport in Memphis. I was working the midnight to 8:00 A.M. shift.

There were three of us working one night: me, another guy, and the girl who worked the counter. The other guy was really picking on the girl.

"Hey, baby! Why don't you and me step into the back for a few minutes."

"Just leave me alone, okay?"

"Come on sweetheart, let me give you a thrill."

She was embarrassed and kept telling him to lay off, but he wouldn't. Finally, I had had enough.

"Hey, hey, hey! Why don't you back off a little bit, okay?"

He made a rather unfriendly gesture. "Shut up, Stanley!"

He left the room, and when he came back, he was carrying a gun.

"I'm just warning you! You stick your nose into my business and I'll blow your head off!"

"Okay." I put my hands up in front of me. "I'm sorry."

He put the gun in his pocket. But at least he was so angry with me that he quit picking on the girl.

A few minutes later, I called Rick to see how he was doing. When Elvis was angry with us, we were both miserable. The first thing I said to him when he answered the phone was, "Hey, Rick! There's a guy down here who wants to blow my head off! What do you think I should do about it?"

The only answer was a loud click as he hung up the phone.

About five minutes later, I was surprised to see a blond blur running across the parking lot toward the office. "Where is he? Where is he?" Rick had fire in his eyes. He was ready to defend his "little" brother. I don't think Rick had ever had a fight in his life. His motto had always been "peace at any cost," or at least that's the way it seemed. I was the fighter, Rick was the peacemaker.

By this time, Rick was so heavily into drugs that he had wasted away to perhaps one hundred pounds.

I thought, *Rick is going to beat somebody up? This I have to see!*

"Where is he?" he asked again.

"He's outside."

The guy was putting fuel into a low-wing prop job, so we went out to confront him. Or, more accurately, Rick went out to confront him, while I went out to watch.

We walked up to the plane, and Rick tapped the guy on the shoulder. "Are you the guy who threatened my brother?"

"Yeah! What are you gonna do about it, punk?"

The next thing I knew, Rick had a greased buck-knife in his hand. He grabbed the guy by the hair and slammed him down against the airplane. He had the knife against the guy's throat. "I'll kill you," he growled through gritted teeth.

"Rick! Rick!" I pulled him off, and the guy struggled to his feet, holding his hand in front of his throat.

"Rick, are you crazy?" I hadn't expected him to pull a knife on the guy. I took the knife away and walked him back to the office. Rick's victim was right behind us.

"I'll get you for this!" he yelled. "I'll have you fired!" He turned to Rick. "And I'll see to it that you go to jail! You Stanley boys think you're such big stuff just because you're Elvis Presley's little brothers. But you're going to regret that you ever messed with me...."

While he was still talking, Rick looked at me. "Deck that____!"

"What?"

"Deck him!"

He was still talking, but I just turned around and popped him on the jaw. He hit the floor and stayed there. I knew I'd lost my job, but it felt good anyway.

Rick and I walked out of the building, got in my car, and drove home.

An hour or so later my boss called. He wanted me to come to the office right now. I walked in, not knowing what to expect. The guy I had hit was sitting there rubbing his bruised jaw, and a heated discussion was underway between him, the boss, and the countergirl. When I told him my version of the evening's events, the girl backed up everything I said. The guy, of course, was claiming that I had provoked him and that Rick had pulled a knife on him for no reason.

After hearing all the evidence, the boss said, "David, I think I understand what happened here tonight. And if he doesn't leave her alone, you have my permission to hit him again."

After that, things were pretty quiet for the next two or three weeks. Then one night I was walking down Winchester Street in Memphis. It was dark and rainy. I heard a car coming up behind me, but I didn't pay any attention. Then somebody yelled my name. The car doors swung open, and five or six guys jumped out and came running at me.

One of them hit me in the face. Another one kicked me. I tried to fight back, but there wasn't much I could do against those odds. Two of them held me while another one hit me in the face again and again. Finally, they all picked me up and tossed me off a bridge. I landed on my back on the grass below. For a minute, I thought I was dead. I could hear my attackers laughing, and then the sound of their car peeling rubber.

Somehow, I struggled to my feet and limped the rest of the way home. Jimmy Marberry was there, and so were Rick and his girl friend.

I was badly bruised and covered with blood. Jimmy was so angry, he wanted to go out right away and track the guys down. The only problem was that I had no idea who they were.

"What did they look like?"

"I don't know," I moaned.

"What do you mean, you don't know?" he demanded.

"I just don't know. It's dark, and it's raining!"

"What kind of car did they have?"

"I didn't get a good look at it."

"We've got to get them for this."

"I promise you, Jimmy ... we'll get them ... we'll get them. Just let me heal first!"

When Elvis found out about it, he reacted the same way Jimmy did. He wanted to get those guys, but I didn't have a single clue as to who they were. I suspected that it might have something to do with the guy at work, but we never did find out.

Whoever they were, whatever made them want to beat up on me, there was one bright side to the whole affair.

"That's enough of this crap!" Elvis snorted. "You're back working for me!" And so I was.

It was smooth sailing between us from that day on. Well, almost, anyway.

The next misunderstanding between us came about because of our parents' divorce. Mom and I were having lunch together at a restaurant in downtown Memphis, and we were talking about the situation between her and Vernon.

Mom was extremely upset at the time, and, in retrospect, I believe she was desperately trying to win back my allegiance. She may have thought she was trying to save my life.

As we talked she began to cry. "David, there are so many things you don't know ... so many things that happened between Vernon and me."

As she talked, I began to get the impression that he had physically abused her. Seeing my mother cry upset me, and thinking that Dad might have hit her was more than I could take.

I ran out of the restaurant, hopped in my car, and broke

the speed limit all the way to Graceland. I found Dad and Elvis in the living room, talking about the next tour.

"David," Elvis said, "how ya doin', buddy?"

Ignoring him, I pointed at Dad. "I'm here to kick your butt!"

Vernon's eyes went cold. "You don't even want to try it, son."

"That's right," Elvis agreed. "You don't even want to try!"

He was right. I didn't want to try. I didn't want to be involved in a fistfight with my father or my brother.

"I'm sorry." I shook my head, which was spinning in confusion.

"You want to tell us why you're so ticked off?" Dad asked.

"I just don't know what to believe," I answered.

"About what?" Elvis asked.

"It's just that Mom is telling me all this stuff, and it's got me upset."

"What kind of stuff?" Dad asked.

The two of us walked into the kitchen while I told him all the things she had said.

"I just want to know what's going on here!"

"Look, David—you grew up in the same house with your mother and me. You tell me what's going on. You tell me if I ever beat her or mistreated her."

"I never saw anything," I said.

"Well?"

"I'm sorry. She just got me upset."

"I understand. And I'm sorry that things didn't work out between your mother and me. But I'm not going to take all the blame for that."

I drove back to the restaurant, where Mom was still sitting at the table waiting for me. The glass of wine I had been drinking was almost full. I picked it up and drank it down in one gulp, and then I slammed the table with my fist.

"Why are you telling me all this garbage? I don't ever want to hear this stuff again!"

Mom looked stunned.

"Mom," I said, "I love you. But there's not a thing you can do to turn me against Vernon or Elvis. You've got to understand that!" Having said my piece, I walked out of the restaurant and left her sitting there.

Later that evening I went back up to Graceland to talk to Elvis.

"Hey, David, we're going to see a really good movie tonight. Why don't you and Angie come on with us?" He acted as if everything were fine, as if I hadn't tried to pick a fight with Vernon earlier in the day.

"Oh, yeah, that would be great," I said, "but I wanted to talk to you about something."

He looked at his watch. "Well, I've got a few minutes. What's up?"

"I want to talk to you about what happened this afternoon."

"Uh huh?"

"I just want to tell you that whatever's going on between Mom and Dad . . . that's between them. As for me, I like my job—I love my job—and I want to keep working for you."

"David, you're understood." He put his arm around my shoulders. "As far as I'm concerned, the situation is over, so let's both just forget about it.

"Besides," he squeezed my left bicep and pretended to be awed by its size, "where in the world would I find another bodyguard as good as you?"

I was relieved that Elvis understood.

"Now why don't you go tell your wife to get ready. The show starts at 1:00 A.M."

Eight

Drugs, Divorce, and an Exposé

I pushed myself away from the table. "That was absolutely delicious." I patted my bulging stomach.

Priscilla smiled. "How about another piece of pie?"

"Are you kidding? I couldn't eat another bite!"

"A cup of coffee, then."

"Sure . . . coffee would be nice. But let me help you."

We both got up to go into the kitchen. As we did so, Mike Stone looked at his watch.

"I hope you don't mind, David, but I have to run. . . . I'm sure you two have a lot of things to talk about anyway."

I shook Mike's hand and thanked him for having me to dinner. I was always embarrassed around him, and I'm sure he felt the same about me. But it was good to be able to see Priscilla again.

I felt a small twinge of something, I didn't know exactly what, as I watched him kiss Priscilla good-bye. I knew that Elvis never had a lack of female companionship. He went through women the way some guys go through razor blades. But that didn't change the fact that Priscilla was the one great love of his life. He would never be over her leaving, and there would never be anyone who could fully take her place in his heart.

It was easy for me to see why. Every time I saw her, I'd realize that I had forgotten how beautiful she was. Even tonight, in a simple cotton dress, looking very domestic, her beauty would take your breath away. It isn't just a physical beauty, either. Priscilla has grace and style.

After Mike left, we went into the kitchen to fix the coffee. Without him there, we would both feel free to talk—and not just the sort of small talk we had been making during dinner.

"I've always liked Mike," I told her.

"I'm glad. . . . David, how's he doing?"

I leaned against the refrigerator and let out a heavy sigh.

"I don't know. Sometimes he's okay. But then. . . ." I stopped in mid-sentence, not really knowing what to say.

"Isn't there anything you can do?"

"Believe me, I've tried." I watched her as she poured the pot of water into her coffee maker. "He really misses you, you know."

She didn't answer, but I saw her biting her bottom lip.

"He probably wouldn't admit it," I continued, "but he talks a lot about you . . . still. He talks like he's mad, and all that . . . but I'm sure it's because he misses you so much."

"Well . . . what about Linda Thompson? What's she like?"

"Oh, she's really neat. You'd like her. She's been real good for him, and I know he cares about her. But. . . ." I stopped because I really wasn't sure where I was going next.

"But what?"

"I don't know, really. I guess it's like that old record of Elvis's, you know . . . 'It's just breaking my heart 'cause she's not you.' "

"David, do you think I did the right thing?"

"About what?"

"You know about what! Leaving Elvis."

I looked around at the tiny kitchen. "This isn't Graceland, is it?"

She laughed. "No, it's not. But I feel like I have more space here than I did there."

"You love him, don't you?"

"Mike? Oh, yes."

"Then I guess you did the right thing."

Priscilla poured our coffee, and we carried it into the living room.

"Priscilla, I don't know what to tell you. You had to do what was best for you, and I understand that. I know Elvis would probably be mad if he knew I came over here tonight. But he's not going to decide how I feel about you. I've always loved you, and I always will love you. I hope you know that."

She reached over and patted my hand. "Thanks for being my friend."

*   *   *

Elvis Presley's life didn't end when Priscilla walked out the door. But for the rest of his life, I believe the divorce was always in the back of his mind, and occasionally would work its way to the front, where it would erupt into violent anger or cause deep depression. Elvis Presley had hundreds of awards attesting to his success, but he had failed when it really counted—in his marriage.

Most of the time, we were still having fun, living the way we always had, tasting life with a sort of reckless abandon. But there were warning signals that the gravy train wasn't going to chug on down the track forever.

For one thing, Elvis was having trouble keeping his weight under control. He was in his late thirties, and the king of rock 'n' roll was developing "middle-age spread." In between tours, his weight would shoot up, and then he'd have to work like crazy to get it off. It had always been easy for him to get into shape before. Now it was extremely hard work.

But still, there were the fun times. Some of the best were when we were involved in our favorite sport—karate.

As I said, Elvis had seen to it that I was trained under some of the best karate instructors in the country, including Bill Wallace, who was a world champion. Elvis was so interested in karate that he bought his own karate studio. He called it Tennessee Karate. When we were home from tours in 1975 and 1976, Wallace and I taught karate there.

When we were on tour, I worked with Elvis on his karate. He was an exceptional student and could have excelled even more in the art if he had had more time to devote to it.

As it was, he was a seventh-degree black belt and plenty tough to handle. Once in Los Angeles, we were driving down the street in one of his Cadillacs. There was a group of men standing in front of a service station, and when we drove by, one of them gave us an obscene salute. Elvis wasn't going to put up with that. He wheeled the car around and drove back to where they were standing, squealing to a stop in front of them.

He jumped out and I was right behind him, in case he needed me. He pointed at the offending party. "Did you shoot me the bird, buddy?"

The guy smarted off, challenging Elvis to do something about it.

"Look man," Elvis responded, "I don't like people talking to me that way."

Instead of answering, the guy lunged at Elvis. Elvis responded with two swift kicks, one to the guy's head and the second to his backside. Before he knew what had happened, he was sitting there on the ground, rubbing his sore jaw. Elvis stood over him, in his karate stance, but the guy made no move to get up, and none of his friends seemed inclined to move in and help him. We waited for a minute or so, then got back in the Cadillac and floored it, leaving a spray of gravel behind as we took off into the night.

Another time in Los Angeles we were sitting at a stoplight, when a woman in the car next to us recognized Elvis.

She jumped out of her car and came running over to ask him for his autograph, which he was happy to give her. But he was still in the process of signing it when the light turned green. The people in the car behind us were angry that we were blocking their way and started leaning on their horn.

Elvis quickly finished signing the autograph, shook the woman's hand, and we were on our way. But the people behind us weren't satisfied. They came up beside us and started coming over, trying to run us off the road. There were several teenagers in the car, and they were leaning out the windows, yelling obscenities at us.

Elvis didn't take that sort of treatment. He pulled out his gun and shot three times into the air. Then he started screaming at them, "Pull over! Pull over right now!" I was sitting next to him, and I leaned over and yelled, "You better do what he says. He'll blow your brains out!"

They believed me and immediately pulled off to the right of the road. We jumped out with our guns drawn and approached their car.

When they realized it was Elvis Presley, they all freaked out.

"Elvis Presley!" the driver yelled. "Hey, Elvis, we didn't know it was you!"

"I don't care who you thought it was," Elvis said, as he put his gun back into his pocket. "You've got no right to go around acting that way!"

He gave them a good tongue-lashing, while they listened quietly. "Yes, sir! Yes, sir!" And then, satisfied that they had learned their lesson, he was ready to forget it and let them go.

Elvis was always quick to pull out his gun, and we lost more television sets that way! If someone came on that he didn't like, he'd just pull out his gun and BLAM! blow the set away. There were several singers that he just did not care for, and if they happened to come on the tube we all knew it was time to buy a new set. (Fortunately, he knew better than to point his gun at someone. It was usually television sets, chandeliers, and other inanimate objects that took the brunt of Elvis's wrath!)

In addition to his karate and his guns, Elvis had an interest in a less violent sport—racquetball. Sometimes we'd drive over to Memphis State University to play a game or two, which I would just about always win. Finally, Elvis had a racquetball court built on the Graceland property. It didn't help his game any!

It was also in 1975 that Elvis bought what he called "the best toy I've ever had." That was his private jetliner, the *Lisa Marie*. Elvis sent Joe Esposito to Tucson because he heard the Arizona city was a good place to buy an airplane.

Joe found a Convair 880, which he could buy for $250,000. He called Elvis and asked him to come out to Tucson to look at the plane.

"Well . . . how much is it?"

"Two-hundred-fifty thousand!"

"And you like it?"

"Yes, but I know you'd like to see it."

"Nah . . . if you like it, that's enough for me. Go ahead and buy it. I trust your judgment."

So Elvis plunked down a quarter of a million dollars to buy an airplane he had never seen.

The jet was flown back to Memphis, and I'll never forget how excited Elvis was when he saw it land. As the giant aircraft came taxiing down the runway, slowly rolling to a stop in front of us, he fell to his knees.

"I can't believe it!" he said. "I've never had a toy like this! This is terrific!"

He was like a little boy—he went in and sat in the cockpit, walked up and down the aisle, and sat in several of the seats.

He wound up spending an additional $600,000 to fix the plane up the way he wanted it, and he hired a crew of four, who were on duty at all times.

The crew quickly became aware of Elvis's spontaneous, spur-of-the-moment life-style. You may have heard the story of how Elvis once decided to fly from Memphis to Denver, just so he could buy some of his favorite peanut butter sandwiches. He gave the crew ninety minutes' notice that time.

It wasn't uncommon over the next couple of years, to have the phone ring in the middle of the night.

"David, get your things together, man, we're going to Vegas."

Life around Elvis had never been suited for long-range planning, and that was especially true once he had the *Lisa Marie.*

He was extremely proud of that airplane.

Once in Baltimore, we arrived for a concert at the same time as the rock group Led Zeppelin. Elvis didn't know much about Led Zeppelin, except that Rick and I thought they were great.

Coming off the *Lisa Marie,* we met Jimmy Page and Robert Plant, two of the leaders of the group, in the middle of the field. As was usually the case, I was awed to meet two of my rock 'n' roll heroes, and they were just as awed to meet Elvis.

As we stood talking, Elvis looked over at their jet.

"I like your 707."

"Yeah?" said Robert Plant. "We lease it from—"

"Oh?" Elvis interrupted. "I *own* mine."

Later on he teased me about it. "See, those guys aren't so heavy. They have to lease their airplane!"

Another time, we were in Los Angeles, but getting ready to fly north for a concert in Fresno. Usually, some of the other guys and I would fly on ahead to set things up. We would make security arrangements, check out the concert site, and do all the other preplanning. We would fly up in a little 440 Convair, and then Elvis would come on in later, aboard the *Lisa Marie.*

This time, as we flew out of L.A. International, a nightmare came true: We lost an engine on takeoff. Everybody on board knew the plane was going down. We all thought we were going to die, but nobody was panicking. J. D. Sumner, who was still drinking heavily at the time, pulled out a fifth of whiskey and started chugging it down.

"If I'm gonna go, I'm gonna go right!" he said.

Everyone else was breaking out the dope, looking for one last high!

The pilot informed us that he was going to try for an emergency landing at an airport in Burbank. It was a rough landing—we bounced a couple of times—then a cheer went up when we finally realized we were safely on the ground.

Immediately one of the guys in the band, Pat Houston, the trumpet player, called out, "There's no business like Fresno business." We all laughed as if that were the funniest line we had ever heard. It was just great to be alive and back on the ground!

There were ten or fifteen guys on board, and as soon as we got off the airplane, most of us ran for the airport rest room. We stayed in there and blew cocaine for a solid hour.

Finally, we got on board another airplane and flew on to Fresno. That night, after Elvis got into town, I went to his room to tell him about our near-disaster.

Just as I got to the part about our emergency landing in Burbank, my nose started to bleed.

Elvis was leaning back in a chair, listening to me. As soon as my nose started bleeding, he leaned forward and slammed his fist on the arm of the chair.

"You been doing a little cocaine lately, David?"

"No . . . not really." The truth was that I was snorting every day, but I wasn't going to admit that. I was also taking amphetamines and barbiturates; sometimes three or four Quaaludes a day.

"What in the world am I going to do with you? That stuff will kill you!"

He lectured me for another ten or fifteen minutes about the dangers of drugs, while I just stood there and listened. Elvis hated drug users, drug pushers, and drugs in general. As I stood there listening to him lecture me, I knew he really didn't realize that he himself was on drugs. The difference was that I took mine for fun; he never did. He only asked the doctors to prescribe for him when he was sick or not feeling well. But over the years the doctors had slowly gotten him to where he was becoming more and more dependent on them—and their medication. The key words here are *dependent on them*. I'm sure Elvis never knew he was addicted. Had he, he would have kicked drugs and the doctors' butts at the same time.

One good example of how doctors made themselves necessary and important in Elvis's life has to do with the sinus problem that Elvis and I both suffered with from time to time. Elvis had once given me liquid cocaine which he honestly thought was sinus medication!

When that happened, we were in Colorado, and Elvis decided I needed some credentials so I could carry a gun. He had had me deputized in Memphis, but he figured it wouldn't hurt to also get a badge from the Denver Police Department.

He made a phone call to the chief of police, who was a friend of his.

"Look, we need to get my little brother sworn in so he can carry a gun legally. I'd like for him to be at least a sergeant."

After he hung up the phone, Elvis turned to me: "Okay, it's all set. We're going to go in today and see the chief, and he'll take care of it. He'll swear you in, take you out to the shooting range, and we'll get your badge."

"Far out!"

At this time my favorite outfit was dirty jeans and tennis shoes, and I had long hair that reached halfway down my back. In other words, I wasn't your typical symbol of law and order.

I also had a bad case of the sniffles.

Elvis lay down on his bed. "We'll go on over there in half an hour or so ... and ... what's wrong, you getting a cold or something?"

"Just my sinuses."

"Oh? I have just the thing for that." He pointed to his "first-aid kit" over in the corner. "Look in there and find a little green bottle."

I did as he asked, found the bottle he wanted, and handed it to him.

"Now hand me a couple cotton balls."

He took the cotton balls and soaked them, using a dropper from the little bottle. Then he put one up each nostril.

"This is something Dr. Nick gave me to help with my sinuses. Maybe you should try some."

"Sure."

He handed me the bottle; I got a couple of cotton balls and did exactly as I had seen Elvis do.

As soon as it hit my nose, I knew exactly what it was: 100-percent-pure pharmaceutical cocaine.

"Elvis," I yelled, "this is pure cocaine!"

"Come on, David," he said sarcastically. "Nick's not gonna give me liquid coke for my sinuses."

So Elvis and I got into the car and drove downtown to the Denver police station, with cotton balls soaked in cocaine stuffed up our noses. By the time we got there, I had such a buzz on that I know my eyes must have been as big around as pizzas!

Elvis couldn't have been much better.

So there we were, talking to the chief of police, a captain from the department, a judge, and the head of the Denver narcotics bureau—and both of us high on cocaine.

I don't know how I passed the shooting test, and the written test was even worse. But somehow I did, and I was sworn in as a sergeant in the Denver Police Department.

I wondered what some of the other policemen were thinking—especially those who had been on the force for five, six years, or more, and who hadn't yet reached the rank of sergeant. Here I was, walking in off the streets, looking like a freak, completely coked out, an instant sergeant!

*　　*　　*

We had come to Colorado from Michigan, where Elvis had performed at the Silverdome in Pontiac. During the final concert there, a man had made an attempt on Elvis's life. He had come out of the crowd with a gun and managed to get pretty close to Elvis before the police got to him. Naturally, Elvis had been extremely upset by the incident, and when he was upset, he would get hyperactive. Sometimes he'd need some medication to calm him down.

In Colorado, he would often ask me to come into his room and read to him to help him fall asleep.

One night, we were sitting and talking while he ate a sandwich. I had already taken a couple of Quaaludes and snorted some cocaine, so I was pretty far gone. Elvis started talking about the guy in Pontiac who had tried to shoot him.

"Why do you think he wanted to kill me, David?"

"He was just a stupid jerk."

"But why did he want to hurt *me*?"

"I don't know."

He took a bite of his sandwich. "Let's call him and ask him why he did it."

I was too far gone to be surprised. "Sure, if that's what you want to do."

It wasn't easy to track the man down, but somehow I was able to do it, and I got him on the phone.

"Sir," I said, "my name is Dave Stanley, and I'm a bodyguard for Elvis Presley—" Before I could say anything else, the guy started laughing. Elvis was sitting next to me trying to hear what the guy had to say, and when he heard the man laugh, he really got angry.

He grabbed the phone out of my hand and started yelling, "Why would you want to kill me, you____! You're going to be sorry you ever messed with me. I'll have you killed right now—I'll have your whole family killed!"

I knew it was his medication talking, so I grabbed the phone away from him. He was fighting to hang on to it, but I finally got it and hung up.

Then he turned his anger on me. "You'd better look at the

bottom of your paycheck and see who it is that signs it! That creep tried to kill me!"

He began pacing around the room, talking to himself. "That lousy_____. I'll kill him! David, you get the jet ready. We're going to fly to Detroit, and we're going to take care of that guy." He was beside himself. Finally, he sat down on the edge of his bed and put his head in his hands. I could feel his hurt.

"David, I'd like to be alone now."

"Oh ... sure ... are you ... going to be all right?"

"Yeah ... yeah, I'm fine. That guy just got me upset, and I think I need to be alone."

"Okay, if you're sure?"

"I'm sure."

I hated to leave him when he was upset like that, but if he wanted me to go, I had no choice but to go.

The next day, Elvis seemed fine. He never mentioned anything about the phone call. Neither did I.

The difference between me and Elvis was that, even though I was abusing drugs, I knew what I was doing, and Elvis didn't. I took drugs because they were fun and made me feel good; Elvis took "medication" because he thought he needed it.

Rick was worse off than either one of us. He was so far gone he could not live without his drugs. I was taking pills and blowing coke, while Rick was mainlining anything and everything he could get his hands on. If he could figure out how to melt it down, he'd shoot it. He was a junkie of the worst sort, to the point where drugs were the most important thing in his life, if not the only thing.

Elvis was constantly on his case about the drugs, but to no avail. Finally, one night we were at the Memphian Theater when a couple of police officers came in. Elvis told me to go find out what they wanted.

"We're looking for Elvis Presley."

"I'm Elvis's bodyguard. Can I help you with something?"

"We just arrested a Rick Stanley. He says he's Elvis Presley's brother—and he's asking for Elvis to come down to the station."

"Well, what's the deal?"

It turned out that Rick and a friend had been at Baptist Hospital, trying to fill some prescriptions that they had forged. The pharmacist asked them to wait while he filled the prescription, and then he called the police.

"Okay, I'll tell him. We'll be right down there."

Elvis was upset when I told him that Rick had been arrested. "Oh, no, what did he do?"

After I told him, he gave a heavy sigh. "Let's go get him."

He didn't say another word all the way to the station. When we got there, Rick was in a holding cell. He sat there, a shriveled up little man, looking like a whipped puppy.

"Rick, how could you do this?" Elvis demanded.

Rick didn't answer. He just looked down at the floor.

"I've never been more disappointed in you." Elvis's eyes were brimming with tears. "You've made a shambles out of our family's name."

"I'm sorry, I. . . ."

"How do you think your mother is going to feel about this? This will kill her!" Elvis shook his head. "Man, I just can't believe you would do something like this."

Then his attitude softened. "Well, we'll talk more about this later. You just hang on, though; we'll have you out of there in a minute."

Elvis went and had Rick released into his custody, and the three of us left the station together. All the way home, Rick kept thanking Elvis and saying how he had learned his lesson—that he was going to lay off the dope from now on. Of course, all those promises were empty ones. If anything, the situation became worse instead of better.

Not too long after that incident, we went out on tour, and Rick and I were staying next door to each other. One night I stopped by his room for some reason. I knocked, but there was no answer. I knew he was in there, so I knocked again, louder. Still no answer. I tried the door—it opened, and I walked on inside. Rick was lying on the floor unconscious.

"Rick, Rick! What did you do?"

I slapped his face, but there was no response. I assumed he had overdosed, and I didn't know what to do. I couldn't very well call a doctor and say that my brother was suffering from a drug overdose! Finally, I decided to get him into the shower. I dragged him into the bathroom, sat him on the floor of the shower, and turned the water on him, trying to bring him around. Finally, the color began to come back into his skin, he came around.

Then I called my mother and told her what had happened.

"Mom, Rick almost died."

"Don't worry about it, son. I know he'll be okay."

"Why, what are you talking about?"

"I don't know. I just felt like something was wrong, so I've been praying for him all day."

In retrospect, maybe it was Mom's prayers that kept us both alive.

*   *   *

I think part of the problem in Elvis's life at that time was boredom. He often told me that he loved performing, and I could tell that it was true. The money was nice, but the real thrill came from getting up in front of an audience and doing a good job entertaining them. But life on the road becomes monotonous, especially when you're singing the same songs night after night, hundreds of times every year.

He needed something new to come along, to revitalize his career and get him excited again.

He was also depressed because his favorite dog, a chow named Getlow, had died. Elvis had always loved animals, especially dogs and horses, but Getlow was his favorite dog ever. In fact, when the dog became sick, we flew him to Boston so a prominent surgeon in that city could treat him. No, not a prominent veterinarian, a prominent *surgeon*. That dog got the sort of medical treatment few people can afford. But his life could not be saved.

Elvis loved that dog, and he cried when it died. It took him weeks to get over his loss.

Then something came along that looked like it would give him that boost he needed so badly. Barbra Streisand, whose talents Elvis had always admired, asked him to consider being her co-star in her newest movie, a remake of the classic, *A Star Is Born*.

This was the sort of movie Elvis had always wanted to make—a movie where he could show that he really had the ability to act. A movie like this could give him a whole new career. If he did a good job in *A Star Is Born*, there would surely be other quality films to follow. Could he still be out on the road rockin' and rollin' at fifty? Highly unlikely. But his serious film career could just be getting started at that time.

A meeting between Streisand and Elvis was arranged. She showed him the script, they traded a few lines back and forth, and everything seemed fine. Elvis was truly excited. But then he took a copy of the script home, so he could read the entire thing over before agreeing to co-star.

What he discovered troubled him deeply. The character he was being asked to play was supposed to commit suicide.

"I don't think I can play this part," he told me.

"Why not?"

"Because this guy kills himself. What kind of a role model is that? I'm supposed to tell people that when you get yourself in a bad situation it's okay to take the chicken way out? I don't believe that."

"But it doesn't really say he did the right thing," I protested.

"I don't know, David, I don't know. I just don't believe in

it, and I don't know if I could play the part of somebody who kills himself."

There was another problem as well. Barbra Streisand was to be the star of the movie, and Elvis would get second billing. Streisand was even going to sing the theme song, "Evergreen."

I don't think the billing bothered Elvis that much, but Colonel Parker wouldn't hear of it.

"The king doesn't take second billing!" he growled.

Finally, Elvis told him to go ahead and turn down the part.

It wound up going to Kris Kristofferson, and it was the beginning of several choice movie roles for him.

Ironically, Elvis really wanted to do that movie. I thought it was a mistake for him to turn it down, and I told him so. Losing the part, even if it was his own decision, was another blow.

It was also at this time, early in 1976, that Elvis was becoming less and less satisfied with the work done by Red and Sonny West. He and Red had been friends for years, but Elvis began to think he was going to have to do something. There were other members of the staff with whom he was dissatisfied, too, and he felt cutbacks were needed.

He decided to retreat to Palm Springs, where he would analyze the situation. He would call everybody in—different groups of people at different times—and get our ideas on what changes were needed. There were all sorts of rumors, and we all were afraid that our jobs were on the line.

One day Sonny West called me. "David, have you heard anything from Vernon?"

"No, why?"

"Well, be prepared, because they're cutting back."

When Elvis called me to Palm Springs, I gave him my honest opinions on who was doing a good job and who wasn't. He seemed especially interested in what I thought about Red and Sonny.

Finally, he told me that there was an almost unanimous

agreement that they were causing more trouble than they were worth. He hated to do it, but he felt that he was going to have to let them go.

On July 13, 1976, he gave both of them their walking papers, along with another security guard named Dave Hebler.

A few months later, when we were in Mobile, Alabama, I received a telephone call from Joe Esposito:

"David, I need you to come up to Elvis's room right away. Something has come up that we all need to talk about."

When I walked into Elvis's room, he was sitting cross-legged in the middle of his bed, holding some papers in his hand. Rick was already there, along with Larry Geller, Charlie Hodge, and Joe Esposito.

As soon as I shut the door, Elvis sighed and said, "They're trying to kill me."

Nobody said anything for a minute, and then Charlie asked, "Who's trying to kill you?"

Instead of answering, he handed the papers he was holding to Charlie. The rest of us gathered around, trying to see what Charlie was looking at. It was an outline of a book about Elvis.

Joe Esposito explained, "It seems that Red and Sonny, along with Dave Hebler, have signed a contract to do a book on their experiences working for Elvis.

I glanced at the title, *Elvis, What Happened?* That said it all to me. This book was definitely not going to be complimentary.

Joe explained that friends in the publishing business had told Elvis about the book. So far, a brief outline was all we had, but we were ordered to find out anything we could and report back to Joe.

Elvis shook his head. "I don't know how those guys could do this to me." He seemed to be almost in a state of shock. He was on the verge of tears.

Over the next few weeks, Elvis was completely absorbed by the book. It was all he wanted to talk about. And, as bits and pieces of information came in, the picture looked worse and worse. There were stories about Elvis's sexual escapades, about his drugs, about his outbursts of temper.

He was convinced that people who read the book would turn their backs on him. Without his fans, what would he be? The answer was nothing—nothing at all. He was worried, too, about those who would be disillusioned by the book. He wanted to be a good role model. He wanted young boys to be able to look up to him as a patriotic, clean-living adult. And this book was going to paint a picture of him as a drug-crazed pervert. The idea was more than he could stand.

One day he called me. "David, get ready, we're flying out to Los Angeles."

"Okay. I'll be ready within an hour."

I didn't ask him why we were jetting off on a moment's notice. I'd find out soon enough. Maybe he wanted a date milkshake or something.

On board the *Lisa Marie*, I found out there was a far more sinister reason for this trip.

"I hope you're ready, David," he snarled. "Because we're going out there to kill Red and Sonny."

"Oh, come on, Elvis. Just forget about those guys!"

His angry stare told me he meant business.

"I'm not going to forget anything. I'm going to kill them . . . with or without your help."

"Okay, okay! I'm with you."

He turned away, walked into his private compartment, and shut the door. I said a short prayer that he would come to his senses before we got to Los Angeles.

We arrived in Los Angeles late that night and went directly to Linda Thompson's apartment in Beverly Hills.

By morning, it seemed my prayer had been answered. He said nothing about Red and Sonny. Instead, he went out shopping for cars—and bought two of them: a black Ferrari for himself, and a little sports model for Linda.

The whole day passed without the book even being mentioned. At midnight, I went to my room, climbed into bed, and breathed a heavy sigh of relief. I soon drifted off to sleep.

Three hours later, I was awakened by a loud crash. Someone kicked my door open and turned on the light. I lay there blinking at the figure standing over my bed, trying to adjust my eyes to the sudden burst of bright light. Who was this heavily armed individual? Some mercenary soldier looking for Central America?

No! It was Elvis! The man was practically covered with weapons—two .45s and a Thompson submachine gun.

"Okay, David, let's go! Get your guns on!"

"Go?"

"We're going to kill Sonny and Red."

"Tonight?"

"Are you coming with me, or am I going to have to do this all by myself?"

"No, no, . . . I'll come. Just give me a minute to get ready." My mind was spinning. How in the world was I going to talk him out of this?

When I was finally ready, we jumped into his black Ferrari and took off down Santa Monica Boulevard. We were flying at more than one hundred miles an hour, and Elvis kept talking about what a terrible thing Red and Sonny had done to him. Red had been his closest buddy since high school.

"How could he do that to me, David? I *loved* that guy."

"Listen, Elvis," I said. "I agree with you that we should kill these guys. But I hope you can get me a color TV for my jail cell."

"That's not funny," he snapped.

"Well, it's not going to be funny when we have to spend the rest of our lives in prison."

He just glared at me, but I kept on talking. "You're so afraid of what people are going to think about you after this book. But I'll tell you something—I'd much rather have Lisa Marie think her daddy had a problem with medication than to know he was a murderer!"

"Shut up! What are you trying to tell me? That you're chicken!"

We were going faster and faster, nearly up to 120.

"I'm not saying we shouldn't do it," I answered. "I'm just telling you what we're up against. Can you imagine someone telling Lisa that her daddy and Uncle David went out and killed three innocent men?"

Elvis began to slow the car down. If there was any way to get to him, it was through his daughter.

All of a sudden he began sobbing, "You're right. I couldn't do it anyway! I loved those guys. How could they do this to me?"

He pulled over to the side of the road and handed me his .45s. "Here. You'd better take these."

"You want me to drive home?"

"I think you'd better."

As we headed for home, I told him, "Elvis, I love you. Don't worry about those guys. Nobody's going to pay any attention to what they say. We both know that their book is just a pack of lies."

"But what if some people believe it? What if my fans don't love me anymore?"

"Well, I love you . . . people who really know you will still love you. And I think you'll be surprised. Hey, nobody expects you to be perfect."

When we got back to the house, Linda Thompson was waiting, nervously pacing the floor. When Elvis and I came through the door, her eyes met mine, and she looked relieved, as she realized our "mission" had been aborted.

Together, we took him to his room and tucked him into bed.

Elvis checks out the screaming crowd at the front of the stage. On drums is Ronnie Tutt, the guitar player closest to Elvis is the famed James Burton.

Elvis had read in the paper that a 'killer' tornado had caused considerable damage in Mississippi, the state where he was born. So he picked up the phone, called the Governor, and asked if he could perform a benefit concert to help the victims. This was the first time he had performed live in the state of his birth in almost 20 years. It is estimated Elvis gave away over $20,000,000 to various charities and to those less fortunate than himself.

Elvis performs before another sold-out show at the Cow Palace in San Francisco.
November 1976.

At the end of each show ten personal bodyguards and fifty policeman would have to come out to keep the girls from jumping on the stage. Here I am keeping a close watch on one girl who has that look in her eye.

June 26 1977, Indianapolis, Indiana. Elvis called his father up on stage to greet the fans. This was Elvis' last concert. To everyone else in the world this is a photo of Elvis and Vernon, to me it is my dad and my big brother.

Sometimes fans in the audience would call out, "You're the king."   When this
happened Elvis would stop the show and reply, "There is only one king, and he is
Jesus Christ." On several occasions he actually stopped the show for several minutes
and read passages from the Bible. Many times Elvis told those of us closest to him that
what he really wanted to do was preach the gospel.

Elvis' personal library of Christian books was unequaled. His books did not just sit on a shelf either, they were dog-eared from so much use. He had his favorite passages underlined in every one of them for easier reference. He took them with him on every tour. Here we are walking in the back door of a Holiday Inn just hours before show time. Part of my job this day was to carry his reading material. In my left hand is one of Elvis' Bibles and a book on the Shroud of Turin.

The beginning of another concert. The King reaches for the microphone. Sometimes it could get pretty wild out there with everyone rushing toward the stage trying to get close to him. For this reason, moments before the start of every concert, Elvis would offer a silent prayer that everyone would have a good time and that no one would get hurt.

Nine

A Swift Downhill Ride

We were in Providence, Rhode Island. Elvis had put on a fantastic show, a show that brought back many memories of the early days. His voice had been great, his rapport with the audience superb. It was a triumph of major proportions.

Elvis knew he had done a good job and he was exhilarated. We were sitting in his suite talking—Elvis, Linda Thompson, and I.

Finally, Elvis leaned back in his chair and yawned. "David, I'm getting kind of tired. Go get Nick for me."

By this time in his life, Elvis never went to sleep without help from his doctor. Dr. Nichopoulos would come in every night and give Elvis something to help him rest for the evening.

I summoned the doctor, and Linda and I excused ourselves. While the doctor tended to Elvis, we walked down to the coffee shop, where we sat for a few moments talking.

Linda was the best thing in Elvis's life now, and I loved her—just as I loved Priscilla. Linda was a tall, graceful beauty, a woman with a good heart who loved Elvis dearly.

Her love had seen him through some very difficult times, and although I knew he loved her, too, he had never been able to make a full commitment to any woman.

As we sat in the coffee shop I was struck by the sparkle in her eyes.

"He was good tonight, wasn't he?" She smiled.

"Yeah . . . he was fantastic. Best show in a long time."

"I think he could do that all the time if it wasn't for—"

"I know," I interrupted. "If it wasn't for his 'medicine.' "

"David, can't you . . .?"

I shook my head. "I've tried. You think he'll listen to me?"

"But maybe if—"

"I'll try, okay? That's all I can say."

I looked at my watch. "Well, it's past my bedtime. Let's go see if he needs anything, and then I'm going to turn in."

When we got back to Elvis's suite, I was surprised to find him in bed, completely out. I knew it takes Quaaludes or Placidyls a little while to take effect. But Linda and I had been gone no more than ten minutes, and he was totally unconscious.

"Good Lord!" I yelled. "What in the world did he give him?"

"See, David!" Linda answered. "It's like this every night. I am so sick of this." Suddenly she was crying. "What are they doing to my Elvis?"

That did it. I was going to confront Dr. Nichopoulos right now. I stormed out of the room and practically ran down the hall to the doctor's room.

I banged on the door. "I want to talk to you!" When there was no response, I reached down and turned the doorknob. To my surprise, the door was unlocked, and I slammed it open so hard it bounced against the wall.

The doctor was standing there half-dressed, as he was in the process of getting ready for bed. I shook my finger at him. "You____, I'm gonna kick your butt. If you think I'm going to let you kill Elvis you're crazy!"

I was yelling at the top of my lungs. Joe Esposito came

running out of his room to see what was going on.

"What are you doing, David?"

"This bum is killing Elvis!" I yelled. Then I turned again to the doctor. "How can you do this?"

He waved his arm at me, as if I were some pesky fly invading a Sunday afternoon picnic. "Go away, son. Go away."

Joe put his arm on my shoulder. "Come on, David. Let's talk about this later. It isn't doing any good now."

"Okay, I'll go. But I want you to know," I told the doctor, "someday you're going to stand in judgment to someone, somewhere, for this. You can't get away with this murder."

Out in the hall, Joe tried to reason with me. "Don't you think Dr. Nick knows what he's doing?"

"Yeah! He's killing Elvis and he knows it."

"Come on, David. You're just upset. He's helping Elvis, not hurting him."

Back in my room, I knew I was right. I knew more about drugs than most of the others did. I knew what they were doing to Elvis, but nobody else could see it.

One other time I had tried to talk to Dad about it.

"Dad, I'm afraid Elvis is slowly being killed with all those drugs."

"No ... no ... you're overreacting."

"Have you seen his pharmacy bill lately?"

"He needs those drugs. He wouldn't take them if he didn't."

That was the attitude held by most of the people around Elvis.

When Elvis found out about my confrontation with Dr. Nichopoulos, he was hot. I thought I was about to get fired, again.

"What in the world were you thinking ... barging in there in the middle of the night, threatening him like that?" he demanded. "You were way out of line. If anything like this ever happens again, you can start looking for another job! I've told you before that you're here to do your job. Other than that, you mind your own business."

He wanted me to apologize to the doctor, but I refused. The only thing that kept Elvis from firing me was Linda's support. She told him that she agreed with me and that her own anger had prompted me to act the way I did.

As far as Elvis was concerned, we were both wrong. What did we want him to do, lie awake all night tossing and turning and then be too tired to perform the next day? If we thought the medication was hurting him we were sadly mistaken. It was the only thing making him strong enough to keep going. He was upset and sorry if Linda and I didn't understand that.

But in Baton Rouge, Louisiana, there was more evidence of what the drugs were doing to him.

"Elvis. Hey, Elvis, wake up, man. Time to get up. The show starts in about an hour!"

We were there for a concert at Louisiana State University. As was usually the case, every ticket had been sold well in advance—it was going to be another packed house.

Elvis's warm-up acts were due to go on stage at 8:00 P.M., with Elvis following about an hour later. These days, he was getting up just in time to get dressed and then head over to the auditorium.

He rolled over and moaned. Then he pulled the pillow over his head.

"Come on, Elvis," I persisted, "we've gotta get rolling!"

He slowly rolled over and faced me. "I'm not going."

"But you have to go."

He turned away from me. "I don't have to do anything. I'm the boss. Now go away and leave me alone."

I wasn't going to give up that easy. "But Elvis, you've got over twelve thousand people in the LSU Coliseum waiting for you!"

"That's too bad, but I'm sick, and I'm not going on tonight."

I went out into the hall and found Joe Esposito. "Joe, Elvis says he's sick and he won't get out of bed."

"What?" Joe looked at his watch. "Oh, man! Well, let's go talk to him."

We went back into the room, and Joe tried to wake Elvis up and get him moving. He didn't have any better luck than I'd had. Elvis was not going to perform, and that was all there was to it.

Joe got on the phone with someone at Concerts West who was packaging the tour, and explained the situation. He talked for a while, and then he put his hand over the phone and said to Elvis, "He says if you don't go on, you can expect to be sued."

Elvis sighed. "Ask him what I can do to avoid that."

Joe talked a few more minutes and then turned back to Elvis. "He says if we check you into the hospital tomorrow, that would do it. But we have to have a legitimate reason."

"What about fatigue?"

That would do it. We'd fly home tonight and book Elvis into Baptist Hospital.

"But what," I asked, "about the thousands of people over at LSU, expecting Elvis to show up any minute?" Foolish question.

"David," Joe said, "go on over there and tell them that Elvis isn't coming."

He summoned a couple of policemen, who would drive me to the LSU campus. All the way there I kept trying to think of what I was going to say. Those people were likely to tear me apart when I ruined their evening.

I arrived backstage just as J. D. Sumner was finishing his portion of the show. The crowd was enthusiastic. The folks were wound up and looking for a good-time, rock 'n' roll evening. The applause was deafening as J. D. took his bow and exited.

Well, here goes, I thought. As I walked out on stage my knees were knocking together and my mouth felt as if I'd been eating chalk.

I looked down at the microphone I held in my hand. I was

holding it so tight my knuckles were turning white. As I looked out at the audience, my carefully planned speech made a quick exit stage left, and I was left standing there without a clue as to what I should say.

"Have you all enjoyed the show so far?" I finally asked.

"Yes!" the crowd roared back.

"Good," I said, "but I'm afraid I have some bad news for you. Elvis Presley will not be here tonight—" Before I could finish my sentence, a loud gasp went up from the audience— a collective shriek. I continued, "He's ill and won't be able to perform," but I don't know if anybody heard me. People were yelling and booing, and several of them tried to rush the stage, though they were held back by a ring of armed security guards.

Several more of the guards formed a ring around me and escorted me out of the building. The people were angry, and they were looking for someone to blame. Because I had made the announcement, I was the one they chose. They were yelling insults and throwing paper cups and other things at me. When we were finally safe in the patrol car, and began to pull away from the auditorium, I slumped down in the seat, weak but relieved that it was over.

The police car took me directly to the *Lisa Marie*. Everyone else was already there, and Elvis was lying in the back of his limousine. Joe, Rick, and I picked him up, carried him up the stairs into the airplane, and we took off for Memphis.

The next day, Elvis checked into Baptist Hospital, with the official reason for his admission listed as fatigue. I knew that he had been working much too hard, and he had also been taking too much medication, as prescribed by Dr. Nichopoulos.

I was angry because I knew he was killing himself, and because I had had to face the hostile crowd in Baton Rouge.

That night I gulped down about twenty Valiums. The next morning, I was still so angry I could hardly think straight. The first thing I did was grab my .357 magnum and blast a few holes in the ceiling. Then I picked up a baseball bat and smashed my expensive aquarium into smithereens.

After that, I went out and wrapped my 280 Z around a telephone pole. I wasn't hurt, but I wound up in the hospital, two doors down from Elvis.

That night, Elvis walked into my room.

"What in the world are you doing here?"

"The same thing you're doing here," I answered sarcastically, "drying out."

I knew that there had been a time when Elvis would have done anything to avoid missing a concert. He loved to be on stage, and he didn't do a single show where he wasn't giving it everything he had. But times were changing. Elvis was slipping rapidly downhill. It scared me, and I didn't know a thing I could do to stop it.

He had developed an "I don't care" attitude. He had lost Priscilla, he was in the process of losing Linda Thompson, and he figured that, once Red and Sonny's book came out, he would lose many, if not most, of his fans. He didn't care that he took too much medication; he didn't care that he was overweight; he didn't care that he couldn't remember the lyrics to many of the songs he had been singing since the mid-fifties—he just didn't care. He felt that he didn't have any more to give.

His attitude was demonstrated by his unwillingness to work. RCA wanted him to record an album to be titled *Live From Elvis Presley Boulevard*. All the musicians and technicians were to come to Graceland, and the album was to be recorded in the den, otherwise known as the Jungle Room.

(The Jungle Room was a rather bizarre-looking room, a place where Tarzan himself might have felt right at home. Among its other peculiarities was a waterfall, cascading down one of the walls into a pond at the bottom. A lot of words have been written about that room, as to why Elvis wanted it that way, but the real reason is very simple. When

Linda Thompson wanted to redecorate the room, I went with them to shop for furniture.

Shopping for furniture was not one of Elvis's favorite pastimes, so the first store we went to, he pointed out some furniture with a jungle motif and said, "Let's get that." So, out of Elvis's impatience, the Jungle Room was born!

One other thing about the room—it was acoustically perfect.)

Twice, all the musicians and technicians were left sitting in the Jungle Room all night, waiting for Elvis, who never showed up. He stayed upstairs in his room. He just didn't feel like recording. Would he come down and record tonight or wouldn't he? There was no way of knowing. All anybody could do was sit and wait and hope for the best. Finally, he did get the album recorded, and he did a good job on it. But it took much longer than it should have.

For a while, it looked as if his time in the hospital was going to straighten him out; or perhaps that was just wishful thinking on my part. There were days when Elvis seemed to have it all together. He would talk optimistically about the future, he would look forward to his next concert tour or his next appearance in Vegas. On occasion he would be the Elvis of old, a charming, kind, and generous man.

One night, about three in the morning, Elvis called me. "Let's go to Vegas."

There were just a few of us—Elvis, myself, Billy Smith, and one or two others. We got the *Lisa Marie* ready, and we were on our way before dawn. We had an absolutely terrific time flying out. We sat on the bed in the back room and watched a Pink Panther movie. Elvis felt good, and we were all looking forward to a wild time in Vegas.

We landed in Vegas in the middle of a light rain. As I opened the back door and watched the ramp being rolled up to the *Lisa Marie*, I thought that the situation presented a perfect picture of Elvis's power. The conditions were such that the jet almost seemed to be glowing against the dark sky, and I thought that we must be presenting an awesome spectacle to anyone who might be watching.

I watched as two Mercedeses came zipping onto the runway and pulled up next to the ramp. Elvis's Las Vegas doctor, got out of one of them and, carrying his medical bag, came running up the steps. I held the door open wide, allowing him to enter.

"Hello, doctor."

"David."

Then I led him back to Elvis's compartment. As we approached the door I could hear Elvis joking with some of the other guys, telling them to take it easy at the gambling tables this time. He was laughing and in excellent spirits.

"Hey, doctor!" he laughed. "Somebody sick or something?"

We were busy preparing to go into the city, so we told him we'd be waiting out in the car. Then we left and closed the door behind us. I had taken some cocaine to keep me awake, but Elvis was perfectly straight, perfectly coherent.

After a few minutes—five at the most—the doctor came walking out of Elvis's compartment.

"Okay, he's going to need some assistance getting off the plane."

Rick, Billy, and I went in to see how much assistance he needed. What we found was a shock: Elvis was totally unconscious. He wasn't groggy, he wasn't a little sleepy, he was gone!

The three of us carried him down the ramp, placed him in the backseat of one of the cars, and drove him to the house where we would be staying. Elvis was asleep for the next three days. He didn't wake up to eat, or to use the bathroom, or for any other reason. He was totally unconscious for three days.

I didn't know what the doctor had given him, but it was hard for me to believe Elvis needed anything that would do that to him. On the trip out, he had been fine. Now he was lying there like someone out of a fairy tale who had taken a bite of poison apple.

I didn't say anything to anyone—they didn't seem to listen anyway, but every time I thought about the situation I wanted to choke someone. Unfortunately, my anger was often directed against my wife. She took the brunt of my sarcastic, spiteful attitude, without realizing that my anger was really meant for the doctors who, I thought, were destroying Elvis, and also for Elvis himself because I thought he should have realized what they were doing to him. Our marriage was hanging together by a thread, and I was not helping the situation.

Then, in November of 1976, Elvis was scheduled to perform for a week in Las Vegas. The day before we were due to fly out of Memphis, I was riding my black Sportster down Elvis Presley Boulevard. I saw a car pulling out into the street, but I thought it was going to go into the turn lane. The next thing I knew, it was coming right at me. There was nothing I could do to avoid a head-on collision. I pulled my legs up on top of the gas tank to avoid getting them crushed. But when the car hit me, I flew up over it and landed under a Mack truck.

The big toe on my right foot was nearly torn off by the impact, and my foot was badly skinned and bruised. I was lucky to be alive and in quite a bit of pain. But the first thing that went through my mind as I lay in the road was, *Now I won't be able to go to Vegas.*

I wound up in the hospital for a couple of days and was on crutches when I finally got to go home. I was angry, and miserable, and generally making life unbearable for Angie.

During that week, Elvis called me three times from Las Vegas.

"How you doin' Dave?" he'd say. "Hey, things are going great out here, but I sure miss you." It was funny, but it was still true, after all these years, a few kind words from Elvis could make you feel terrific.

During his last call, he asked me if I could meet the *Lisa Marie* when it came back to Memphis.

"Well, I guess so," I told him, "but I'm still on crutches."

"Just try to be there, okay?"

So, when the plane landed, there I was, still thinking about all the good times I had missed. The guys were whooping it up as they left the plane. They had had a great time, and everyone was feeling good.

Finally, out came Elvis.

"David, buddy, you made it!" He playfully rubbed my head. Then he stuck a piece of paper into my hand.

"What's this?"

"Your bonus."

"But I—" I started to protest.

"I know," Elvis interrupted, "you're going to tell me that you didn't earn it. Well, David, you may not have been there physically, but you were there in spirit. You deserve it!"

"Okay, if you insist," I said, tucking the check for twenty-five hundred dollars into my shirt pocket.

Coming up behind Elvis was a pretty young girl, perhaps my age—maybe a bit younger.

"David, I want you to meet somebody. This is Ginger Alden."

After he introduced us, he winked at me and whispered, loudly enough for her to hear, "I think I'm in love."

From the airport, we all went to Graceland, where Elvis and I had a chance to talk alone.

"What do you think of her, Dave?"

I started to say, "She's kind of young for you, isn't she?" but thought better of it. After all, maybe she was just what he needed. "She's really nice," I said, "a real fox!"

He smiled. "I think I'm going to marry her. What do you think?"

"I don't know ... do you love her?"

"I think I do."

I laughed. "Well, don't marry her until you're sure."

Elvis was up—happy and excited—but if I thought Ginger

Alden was going to change his life-style, I was dead wrong!

In Houston at the Summit, he went on stage even though he was totally exhausted. The concert lasted for fifty-five minutes, and he talked for forty-five of them.

"This is a good song, ladies and gentlemen. I've always loved this song . . ." and on and on and on.

Near the end of the concert, he was singing "Love Me Tender," and Rick and I were off to the side watching him.

"Rick!" I said, "if he gets any closer to the edge. . . ."

I didn't have to finish the sentence. Rick knew exactly what I was talking about. While he was singing, he had started rocking back and forth, lost in his own twilight zone. As he rocked, he was coming closer and closer to the edge of the stage.

Finally, we knew we had to do something. Rick and I walked out and, each taking an arm, walked him back to the center of the stage.

"Elvis," I whispered, "are you gonna be all right?"

He looked at me with glazed eyes. "Where am I?"

"You're on stage," I exclaimed, "in front of nineteen thousand people!"

Amazingly, the audience seemed to love Elvis's show. He could have just stood there for an hour, letting the audience look at him, and they would have loved it. But it was obvious to those of us who knew him: Something was terribly wrong with Elvis.

Coming off the stage that night, he missed a step and fell hard—right on his posterior. When Rick and I came to his assistance, he lashed out at us. Why had we come on stage and interrupted his act? Why had he fallen down? Everything was our fault. We were both dumb and stupid.

"You can't talk to me like that!" I yelled back. "I'll quit!"

"Go ahead! It won't be the first time!"

But for some reason, I didn't quit. I suppose it was because I knew that now, more than ever before, Elvis needed his friends.

The next morning's newspapers carried reviews of Elvis's

concert, and the critics were not kind. What hurt even more than their harsh words was the knowledge that they were right.

Things didn't improve a great deal after that, either.

We were hearing more and more about the stories that were going to be included in *Elvis, What Happened?* and Elvis could hardly stand it.

In his dressing room in Las Vegas, he cried as he told me, for what must have been the tenth time, that the book would destroy him.

"I don't know why they want to say all those things about me. They're all lies. You know that don't you, David?"

"Well, why don't you prove they're wrong?" I challenged him. "Get rid of all this medication, once and for all!"

"But you don't understand. How many times do I have to tell you, I only take what I need?"

*   *   *

On his good days Elvis would talk enthusiastically about the future. He bought Ginger a huge diamond engagement ring and told her she made him happier than he had ever been in his life. She would feel good; maybe life was going to change, and things would be great. But then he'd go back to his medication and his bed.

Ginger and I spent a lot of time together, simply because we were the same age. Elvis would be zonked out, unconscious, and Ginger and I would sit and talk about things—mostly about music. We'd talk about the latest album by Paul McCartney, or a concert tour by Chicago or the Eagles.

Sometimes, Ginger would go into town by herself when the life-style around Graceland started to make her crazy.

Elvis was jealous of Ginger. She was young and pretty, and I'm sure he felt that she needed more attention than he was able to give her. He knew she went out on her own sometimes and asked me to keep an eye on her.

I promised him that I would, but I knew her well enough to know that she wasn't cheating on him. If anything, I understood her need to get out and have some fun.

On one occasion he told me to stop her from going out.

"Now, how am I supposed to do that?"

"I don't know. You think of something—that's why I pay you."

"Well I could always slash her tires." I said it as a joke, but Elvis didn't take it as one.

"That's not a bad idea. She can't be going anywhere if her tires are flat."

"I'll see," I sighed. But I never did slash her tires. I just reassured him that she loved him and that I knew she wasn't interested in anybody else.

Back out on the road, Elvis continued to pack them in, even though the reviews were getting worse and worse. Critics were wondering out loud what in the world had happened to him. They were suggesting that Elvis was through, that it was time to hang up his rock 'n' roll shoes and find another line of work. What they didn't consider was that Elvis had been giving himself unselfishly for more than twenty years, and they had always criticized him for one thing or another. They'd been saying he had no talent, couldn't sing, was vulgar, had no staying power, and other such things ever since he had first sprung onto the public scene back in 1956. So who listened to them? Nobody.

All they could see was that he would launch into one of his standards and then forget the words. He'd pull a piece of paper with the lyrics on it out of his pocket.

"I hope y'all don't mind if I read the words to this one," he'd say. "I've always had trouble with this song!" He tried to make it a joke, to dismiss it with a cavalier attitude, as if the only reason he didn't know the lyrics was that he didn't care enough to have them memorized. The truth was that he simply couldn't remember them.

He would be singing "Are You Lonesome Tonight" and get to the part where he was to talk to his absent sweetheart.

This was an emotional song, intended to break hearts. But Elvis would turn it into a comedy. "Gee, I sure wish I could remember what I was supposed to say next!"

By this time, I knew beyond any doubt that he was dying. I talked to Jimmy Marberry about it.

"If things don't change," I said, "Elvis will be dead inside of six months."

Jimmy agreed with me. "You're right, David. And if you don't change your life-style, you will be, too."

He knew that my anger and depression were growing worse and worse. I was turning more and more to street drugs myself. I knew Elvis was in bad shape, and so was Rick. But I couldn't see what Jimmy saw—that I, too, was rapidly sliding downhill.

I preached at Elvis about his medication, but I didn't listen to my own sermon. Elvis preached at Rick about drugs, but didn't take his own advice. And so it went.

Somewhere along the road, at one of his concerts, a woman in the audience had something she wanted to give to Elvis. Elvis came over to the side of the stage, shook her hand, and accepted the Bible she handed to him.

Then he stood there in the spotlight, holding the Bible.

"I want to read to you for just a minute," he said. The audience grew deathly quiet; not even a whisper was heard.

Elvis flipped over to John 3:16. "For God so loved the world, that he gave his only begotten Son, that whosoever believeth in him should not perish, but have everlasting life."

Finishing that, he turned quickly to the Twenty-third Psalm. As he read, "Yea, though I walk through the valley of the shadow of death, I will fear no evil," I could feel his emotion. He wasn't being showy or pretending to act like a preacher. He was reading those words with feeling. I didn't know whether he was trying to impart those words to his audience or claim them for himself.

Whatever the truth was, his audience sat enraptured, hanging on every word.

175

When he finished reading, he turned to the musicians behind him. "I want to sing 'How Great Thou Art.' "

The critics said Elvis was over the hill and that his voice was gone, but I had never heard him sing the way he sang that song. He sang it with every bit of energy, with every bit of emotion he had.

From my vantage point I couldn't be sure, but when Elvis finished the song, I thought he was crying.

I know I was.

Ten

The King Is Gone

In 1977 my world fell apart.

The first casualty of the year was my marriage.

Early that year, Angie had gone on vacation with us to Hawaii. Even though the tour was okay, things just didn't seem right. She was distant, withdrawn, as if she were always thinking that she'd rather be somewhere else.

After Hawaii, she went back to Tennessee. My calls home confirmed my suspicions.

"Angie, I love you."

"Thank you."

Thank you? What kind of response was that? When I told her I loved her, I expected her to say, "I love you," right back to me.

"Angie . . . is something wrong?"

"No, no everything's fine. Don't worry about it."

But I did worry about it, because, in spite of the way I acted, and in spite of the way I had treated her, I really loved her. I honestly hadn't meant to treat her so poorly—I just didn't know any better.

When we finally arrived back in Memphis, Angie was waiting at the airport. When I embraced her she seemed rigid and cold. When I tried to kiss her she turned her face away.

"David," she sighed, "we have to talk."

I could feel my mouth going dry. She didn't have to tell me. I knew already that I had lost her.

We sat down together, and right there in the airport waiting area, she told me that our marriage was over.

"I've found someone else, David. I'm leaving you."

"But Angie, I. . . ."

"I'm sorry, David. But I just got fed up with all your promises. I didn't mean to fall in love with someone else, but I did. And it's him I want to be with . . . not you."

Then she told me that she had already moved her things out of the apartment. She was leaving immediately for Nashville. She'd be staying with her parents for a while, trying to get her mind clear.

All I could do was sit there. I had nothing else to say.

Maybe Elvis could help me. Surely, a man of his experience could tell me how I could win her back. As soon as I could, I'd talk to him and find out what to do.

That night Elvis and I were sitting in the TV room at Graceland.

"Elvis, I've lost my wife," I said.

"I'm sorry, David. But I've seen it coming."

"But I love her. I don't want her to leave!"

He leaned back and put his feet up on the coffee table. "I guarantee, you, Dave-O, there's a well-built eighteen-year-old out there just waiting for you!"

I couldn't believe it. That sort of talk wasn't making me feel any better. It was Angie I wanted. Not somebody else.

I finally decided that I would go to Nashville, stay there, and do whatever had to be done to win Angie back. I'd show her that I could change and that I could keep my promises.

I'd treat her tenderly and make her fall in love with me all over again. After all, she had said she needed some time to clear her mind. That meant there was still hope that she would change her mind.

So that's exactly what I did. I went to Nashville, where I spent the next several days trying to talk Angie into coming back. I begged and pleaded, told her I didn't know if I could go on without her, and did everything I could think of to show her that I loved her.

My persistence paid off, and she finally agreed to give it another try. She was still in love with someone else and was coming back reluctantly, but she figured our marriage deserved one more chance. She would come with us on our next tour, and we'd see if we could work things out.

Our reconciliation lasted three days.

On that third day, we were in Louisville, Kentucky. We walked into a restaurant and ran right into Brenda, a girl I had spent most of my time with on one of our recent tours.

"David, honey!" She ran up and grabbed me, planting a big kiss on my lips. "I've been looking for you. We're going to have a great time!"

Angie turned around and walked out, leaving me standing there. There was nothing more I could do. Brenda had confirmed all of Angie's suspicions about my life on the road.

She went back to our room, packed her things, and was on a plane back to Nashville the next morning.

After she left, I went out in front of our hotel and stood on the banks of the Ohio River. I took my wedding ring off and threw it, as far as I could, out into the water. It barely made a splash when it hit. I really had been trying, at least lately, and all of my efforts to save my marriage were gone, just like that.

Although I was heartbroken over Angie's departure, I quickly had to get my mind back on business. We had concerts to organize and a TV special to prepare for.

CBS had decided to do a special featuring Elvis in concert. He was anxious to do the show, and yet he was worried about it, too. He was at his heaviest ever—over 250 pounds, and he knew he didn't look good.

He desperately wanted to give a good performance for the nationwide audience, but was afraid he couldn't.

It was more and more apparent to me that Elvis was not going to be around much longer, and I think he knew it, too. He wanted to go out with a bang, not with a whimper. He didn't want to be seen on national television as an aging, overweight has-been. He wanted to be the king.

During this time, Elvis was also going about trying to get his house in order. Wherever there were hurts, or he felt he had done someone wrong, he wanted to make it up.

We were taking a few days' rest at his house in Los Angeles when he caught me by surprise.

"Call Priscilla for me, David."

"Why?"

"Tell her I want to see her."

He had seen very little of Priscilla over the last couple of years. He talked to her from time to time—especially regarding Lisa Marie, who usually spent her summers with her dad at Graceland—but they hadn't visited face-to-face.

"Okay, sure, if you want me to."

I picked up the phone and called her. She seemed surprised that Elvis wanted to see her, but said it would be fine. We could come to her house whenever we wanted. She'd be home most of the day.

Elvis wanted to go right away, so we hopped into his Ferrari and drove to Priscilla's house in Beverly Hills.

When we got there Elvis made it clear that he wanted to talk to her privately. So the two of them retreated to a back room, while I stayed in the living room, thumbing through some magazines. I don't know how long they were back there talking, perhaps twenty or thirty minutes, but finally Elvis came out by himself.

He smiled at me and said, "Everything's okay now."

"Good."

On the drive back to Elvis's house, he didn't say much. I wanted to ask him what was okay, but I didn't. I figured if he wanted to tell me what he and Priscilla had been talking about he would. And if he didn't want to tell me, then I knew better than to pry.

When we got back home Elvis seemed totally drained. He sat on his bed, holding his head in his hands.

"Thanks, David."

"Can I get you anything?"

"No, that's all right. I just appreciate you being here with me. You know, I love you and Billy and Rick. It's important to me that you guys know that. I haven't always shown it, but it's true."

"I've never doubted it for a minute," I told him. Then, going into my karate stance I teased him, "Well, maybe there've been a couple of times!"

On the last tour, Elvis seemed to be trying very hard not to do anything wrong. He was polite to the point of being deferential, trying to wait on us instead of the other way around.

"David, is there anything I can get you? Anything you need?"

"Can't think of a thing."

"Well, if you do need anything, you let me know."

What in the world had come over him? I didn't know.

On to Rapid City, South Dakota, and the CBS concert. The date was June 21, 1977. It was to be Elvis's last shot at the world.

Standing backstage, waiting for the concert to begin, Elvis was nervous and jittery. It was like he wanted to get out there on stage and get it over with. He looked down at himself and shook his head. He didn't like what he saw.

He turned to Rick, who was standing beside him. "I

may not look very good tonight, but I'll look great in my casket!"

Later, Rick and I talked about that comment. What had he meant? Was it some sardonic joke or a premonition?

*　　*　　*

Back home in Memphis, the summer days were hot and lazy, and Elvis spent most of his time in bed. If we could get him out to do something, anything, we felt that we had achieved something. There were occasional games of racquetball—and once or twice we talked him into riding motorcycles. But most of the time, you couldn't get him to budge from the bed. He was forty-two years old, going on ninety.

My mind was still predominantly on Angie. I hadn't yet given up and had embarked on another mission designed to win her back. I admitted that I had been wrong in the past, but told her that was no reason we couldn't work things out in the future. I even enlisted Elvis's help. If Angie would agree to come back to Memphis to give it another try, Elvis would serve as our marriage counselor. We could sit down with him and talk out all of our problems, and he'd make suggestions.

He wouldn't be on my side, and he wouldn't be on Angie's side. He would try to be fair and suggest ways we could both improve our marriage.

I don't think she wanted to do it. But once again, my persistence wore her down. She finally agreed to come back for one more try. It wouldn't hurt to at least talk to Elvis and see if he could help us patch up our differences. But if it didn't work out this time, that was it. She was not going to keep going back and forth, like some sort of human teeter-totter.

We sat in front of Elvis and poured our hearts out. He listened and sympathized and made suggestions, many of which were excellent. Elvis had learned something through the loss of his own marriage, even if he was having a hard time applying it to his own life.

"Angie," he concluded, "David knows that he hasn't been the best husband in the world. He's told me that. He also knows now that you're the most important thing in his life. He wants to make the marriage work. I hope you'll agree that it's worth another try."

Even now, Elvis was a terrific salesman. Angie was convinced. She promised that she would give it her best shot.

As we got up to leave, Elvis asked me if he could speak to me for a minute in private. "Nothing, really, Angie, just a little business matter we need to clear up."

As soon as she closed the door, Elvis reached out and grasped my shoulder. "David," he said, "I'm sorry, but she's gone."

"But she just said—"

"I know what she just said. But she didn't mean it. I hate to have to tell you this, but you might as well forget about her right now. Your marriage is over."

"Uh . . . I . . . ."

"There is nothing you can do. Her heart is somewhere else. She's not going to stay."

Elvis was right. Angie's stay lasted only a few days. By the middle of August, she had gone back to Nashville. I was determined, once again, that somehow I could win her back.

My persistence was brought about in part by my worry about Elvis. I was afraid and needed someone to lean on. Elvis was deteriorating in front of me, and it was a hard thing to take. I hadn't been there for Angie the many times when she needed me, and now the tables were turned. I needed her desperately, and she wasn't there for me.

*　　*　　*

August 13, 1977, was a Saturday, and I was on duty. Three days later, we were set to head out on another long tour. Elvis was down, but not as far down as I had seen him. He was tired, but still seemed to be looking forward to getting out on the road again. He talked about recapturing some of that old magic.

I sat with him for a few minutes before it was time for him to get ready for bed, and we watched television and talked. We talked about a lot of things, but mostly about Angie. I would be off the next two days, and I was planning another of my many trips to Nashville, to try to win her back.

"David, you're going to have to get over her. You have to get on with your life."

My marriage hadn't been the only one to fail. Very few of the men around Elvis were able to maintain lasting marriages. Elvis and Priscilla were divorced, and over the next few years it seems as if almost everyone else in the group followed suit. But I wasn't giving up.

"I'm not ready to quit trying," I answered.

He smiled. "That's one of the reasons you've always been such a good bodyguard. You have the heart of a bulldog—you don't ever give up."

As the light from the television flickered on Elvis's face, I was struck by how tired he looked—tired and strangely sad. His face was puffy, and his eyes were devoid of that mischievous fire that had always made them seem to sparkle. I would have taken him for someone who had worked all his life in a factory or a coal mine—not for the king of rock 'n' roll, and certainly not for the most famous entertainment figure of the twentieth century.

As I sat there with him, I couldn't help but think about how much I loved him. I thought he was the greatest guy in the world, and it scared me to see what was happening to him. I wanted to tell him how I felt, but didn't know how. So we sat there for a few minutes in silence.

"Why don't you shut that thing off," he said, finally. "I think it's about time for me to get to bed."

"Are you going to need me tonight?"

"No, no . . . Ginger's here. She'll be around. You might as well get a head start on 'Mission Impossible.' "

"Mission impossible?"

"Talking Angie into coming back."

"Oh."

He laughed. "Now don't get bent out of shape. I was just teasing. You go bring her back!"

"You think I'm being stupid—?"

Before I could finish the sentence, his hand was on my knee. "Believe me, David. I understand."

"Well, if you don't need me, I guess I'm gonna head on out of here. But I'll see you in a couple of days." I stood up to go.

Elvis shook his head. "No, David. No, you won't see me in a couple of days."

"I won't?"

"The next time I see you, it will be in another time . . . another place. On a higher plane."

I sat back down. "I'm afraid you've lost me. I don't know what in the world you're talking about."

He sighed. "David . . . you won't ever see me again . . . alive."

"Hey, man, don't talk that way!"

He reached over and took my hand.

"I'll save a place for you. You can be sure of that."

I didn't know how else to react, so I tried to make light of it. "Okay, Elvis." I flashed him a big smile. "That'll be fine. I'll see you there."

I stood up to go again, and the next thing I knew, Elvis had me locked in a bear hug.

"Good-bye, David. I love you." He was crying.

"I love you, too, man."

He let go of me and began to wipe his eyes.

"Hey, listen, maybe I ought to stay here for a while."

"No, you'd better go. I'm all right."

"Are you sure?"

He nodded. "Okay," I said, and turned to leave. I opened

the door and then turned, standing in the doorway, and pointed at him. "I *will* see you on Tuesday. And it's going to be the best tour you've ever done!"

That was the last time I ever saw him alive.

I went downstairs and sat in the den for a while. I didn't know what to do, and I hated to leave him. Why had he been talking like that? Maybe it was those mystical books he was always reading. Maybe it was the fact that his last few records hadn't exactly set fire to the sales charts.

I waited for an hour or so and then went back upstairs and put my ear to his door. I didn't hear anything unusual, so I went back down to the TV room and watched an old movie.

After that I went back upstairs and listened at his door again. This time, I heard snoring. Good. Everything was all right.

I went downstairs, through the den, and out the back door. I got in my car, put the key in the ignition, and sat there for a few more minutes, thinking. Elvis had me shook. Why did he have to talk that way?

I exhaled sharply. I just had to put it out of my mind and get on with the task at hand. Right now, that task was winning Angie back.

Tuesday morning, August 16, I arrived back in Memphis an utter failure. Angie wouldn't come back and that was all there was to it. After all this time, it was beginning to dawn on me that the marriage was over. I was glad we were going out on tour tonight. It would be good to get away from the depression that seemed to surround Graceland lately. It would be good to see some different places and some new faces. I was planning on having a ball.

I was due to go on duty at noon. When I got to Graceland, Rick was just getting ready to go off duty, and he looked terrible. Those days, Rick looked terrible most of the time because of his drugs—but that day he looked especially bad.

"Golly, Rick," I teased him, "what happened to you? You get run over by a steamroller or something?"

"Nah . . . just kind of a bad night."

"Why, what happened?"

"Oh, nothing really. Just a bad night for me. Except Robyn called."

"Again?"

Robyn Moye had known Rick since high school. For some reason, she had taken him on as a reclamation project. Robyn was a born-again Christian who lived in Florida. She knew Rick was a druggie, and she was always calling to tell him that he could straighten out his life by turning it over to Jesus Christ.

"Well, Brother Rick," I teased him, "she'll have you marching in the band and singing 'Onward Christian Soldiers' in no time at all."

Rick didn't seem to get the joke. He was serious as he said, "She keeps telling me how I need to start living for Jesus. I was talking with Elvis about it last night, and he thinks she's right. He told me it was high time we all start living for Jesus."

I quickly changed the subject. "Speaking of Elvis, how is he? He was in a pretty strange mood last time I saw him."

"He's doing okay I guess . . . a little weird. He wanted me to pray with him last night."

"Pray with him?" I was flabbergasted.

"Yeah. He asked God to forgive him for all the things he's done that he shouldn't do. And then he asked that God would help him do better in the future."

"Wow!"

"By the way," Rick asked, "how'd it go with Angie?"

I rolled my eyes. "Shhhhh . . . don't ask."

"Hmmm. Sorry. Well, I'm going to go cop a few z's. Elvis doesn't want you to wake him up until four."

After Rick left, I stepped into the poolroom. I figured I'd play a few games before it was time to get Elvis. But I hadn't played too long when Ginger's niece, Amber, appeared in the doorway and told me something was wrong with Elvis.

She was followed by Lisa Marie, who said, "David, my daddy's sick!"

My first inclination was to pick up the phone and call Baptist Hospital, warning them that Elvis might be on his way in. But Lisa was impatient. "Come on David, my daddy's sick and you've got to help him." At that time, I suddenly realized that an ambulance was pulling into the Graceland driveway. Someone had already called the ambulance. For the first time, it hit me that Elvis must be worse off than I had suspected.

I ran up the back stairs and got to Elvis's bedroom at the same time as Joe Esposito and Al Strada.

We walked into the bathroom, where we found Elvis face-down on the floor, his knees drawn underneath him.

I went up to him and shook him gently. There was no response. We grabbed him and rolled him over. I was not prepared for the sight that greeted me. Elvis's face was swollen and black, and his tongue was sticking out of his mouth.

By this time, Vernon had come into the room.

"Oh, no!" he wailed. "My son! My son is dead!"

"No, Dad. He's not dead. He's gonna be all right!"

Vernon was clutching at his chest, and I knew he was about to have a heart attack. Fortunately, his girl friend, Sandi Miller, was there for him to lean on. If she hadn't been there, I honestly think he would have collapsed on the spot.

Charlie came in and started yelling at Elvis, "Don't die! Please don't die!"

He began to give Elvis mouth-to-mouth resuscitation, while I massaged his chest. I noticed, though, that his chest was turning blue, as blood had already been seeping into the chest cavity.

Suddenly, the paramedics came rushing into the room. Charlie and I got out of the way, and they went to work on Elvis. They ran tubes down his mouth and started administering electric shock. Elvis's body was literally bouncing off the floor, as they tried to get his heart started again.

Vernon took my hand and placed it on Elvis's knee. "My son's dead!" he wept. "Feel how cold he is!"

I couldn't believe this was happening. I felt like I was in a bad dream. I had always known that Elvis was going to die. I had told other people that the end was coming—but when it came, I just couldn't believe it.

One of the paramedics looked around. "What happened here?"

"I think it's a drug overdose," I answered. This was no time to play games.

Finally, the paramedics decided they had to get him to the hospital.

"Help me get him on the stretcher," Joe yelled at me. So I grabbed his shoulders and helped Joe lift him onto the stretcher. I grabbed one end of the stretcher, and the paramedics got on the other end. As we were maneuvering our way out of the room, Al Strada came up and grabbed one of the corners I had been carrying. At 255 pounds, it was not easy getting Elvis down the stairs and out of the house.

As Al and I carried him down the front steps of Graceland, our eyes met. We both knew he was gone. There was no doubt about it. Whatever they were planning to do at the hospital was useless.

We put Elvis in the back of the ambulance, while Lisa was screaming, "My daddy's dead! My daddy's dead!"

Al and Joe got in the back of the ambulance with Elvis, and I started to get in, too. But then I saw Dr. Nichopoulos's gold Mercedes come flying up the driveway. He squealed to a stop, jumped out of his car, and came running toward the ambulance. Instinctively, I jumped out to make room for him. As the doctor climbed in, I slammed the doors shut, and the ambulance roared off down the driveway, siren screaming and lights flashing.

I stood there watching it go. Then I went back through the house and out the back door to the carport, where my 280 Z was parked. Coming out the back door I saw Elvis's cousin

Billy Smith. He had arrived just as the ambulance was leaving.

"What's going on here?" he asked.

"Elvis is sick. Well, Billy . . . I think . . . I think he's dead!"

"Oh, my God!" Billy's face went white and his hands began to shake.

We jumped in my car, and I gunned it down the driveway. At the Music Gate, we met several other employees just coming on duty.

They wanted to know where we were headed in such a hurry and I told them that I thought Elvis was dead.

We turned right on Elvis Presley Boulevard and doubled the speed limit all the way to Baptist Hospital. We pulled up in front of the emergency room and ran inside. Joe, Charlie, and Al were standing in the waiting room talking to a doctor. He led us into an area that was normally off limits to visitors and told us he would be back with us just as soon as he had something to tell us.

We sat in there, listening to the hospital noises. We heard metal clanging and the buzzing of electronic equipment. Occasionally, we could hear the muffled voices of the doctors as they worked on Elvis. Even though all of us knew Elvis was dead, we began to hope that maybe a miracle would occur. Perhaps he wasn't as bad off as we had thought.

We sat there for another five or ten more minutes. And then Dr. Nick came in.

We all jumped up and looked at him, searching his face for some sign of hope. Instead, he shook his head.

"He's dead."

Immediately, Joe went into his business mode. "Okay, we're going to have to let everybody know." He and Dr. Nick began to talk about arranging a press conference.

While all that was going on, I walked out of the hospital, got in my car, and headed for Graceland. I didn't really know what I was going to do when I got there. I was operating on automatic pilot.

Just before I got to Graceland, a news bulletin came on the radio.

"This word just in ... Elvis Presley is dead. The famous singer died today at Baptist Hospital of an apparent heart attack."

When I heard it announced on the radio, that made it real. I pulled over to the side of the road and bawled like a baby.

When I finally got back to Graceland, the first person I saw when I walked in the house was Rick. He was as white as a sheet and shaking all over. I could hear Vernon in another room, crying and saying over and over, "Oh, Elvis! My son, my son!"

Several of my aunts and uncles were with Vernon, and they were all crying and carrying on.

I looked at Rick and said, "All we have now is each other, Rick. He's dead."

"Those____!" He screamed. "Those____killed him!" He was referring to Red and Sonny. Then he screamed at the top of his lungs, "I can't believe it!" and took off running down the driveway. I didn't know where he was going, and I'm sure he didn't either.

I got back in my car and drove to my apartment. Jackie Stovall had heard the news on the radio; he was sitting on his motorcycle in front of the apartment waiting for me.

I walked up to him. "Elvis is dead," I said.

"I know, I heard. I'm sorry."

I stood there for a minute, neither one of us knowing what else to say.

Finally, Jackie spoke. "What are you going to do now?"

"I don't know. Get drunk, I guess."

"Sounds like a good idea to me."

"Let's go over to Arilla and Shelley's house."

Arilla and Shelley were close friends of ours. They were hairdressers who had cut Elvis's hair in Memphis. When Arilla answered her doorbell, she had tears in her eyes. She already knew about Elvis.

"Can we come in?" I pleaded. "We thought maybe you'd like to help us drown our sorrows."

"Sure, come on in."

The rest of the afternoon was spent doing just that—trying to drink away the pain. And that was very hard to do.

Later that evening, after darkness fell across Memphis, I went back up to Graceland to see if there was anything I could do. Specifically, I was hoping I could do something for my dad. But he was inconsolable. All the other guys had thrown themselves into the task at hand, getting ready for the funeral, handling the publicity, and dealing with the public.

Priscilla was on her way in from the Coast on board the *Lisa Marie*, which had been flown out to pick her up. Many of Elvis's friends and acquaintances were calling to express their sympathy and to say they would be in town for the funeral.

Outside Graceland, there was a horrendous mob scene, with thousands of people milling about up and down Elvis Presley Boulevard. People were hanging all over the Graceland gates. Even though I knew they were sharing my grief, and they were truly saddened by Elvis's death, I was still angry, because the atmosphere seemed so bizarre, more fitting for Mardi Gras than for the death of my big brother. Why couldn't they just go home and let us be alone in our sorrow?

Finding that I was of no use to anyone at Graceland, I went back to Arilla and Shelley's house and began my drinking and doping in earnest. My years on the road had taught me well: Nothing was so big or so painful that you couldn't hide from it with either drugs or alcohol.

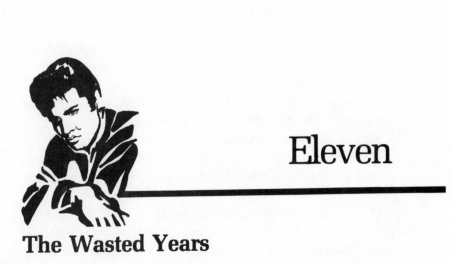

Eleven

The Wasted Years

The next few days were very strange. The mob scene around Graceland continued. One young girl was hit and killed by a car on Elvis Presley Boulevard. Hearing about her death only added to our sense of loss and grief. We knew that Elvis's death had indirectly caused her to lose her life.

The way the crowds were behaving, we were afraid there would be other tragedies.

Elvis's body lay in state in the foyer at Graceland. When the mansion was opened to the public, so people could come and view the body, only eighty thousand people were allowed through the house during a two-hour period. Another couple hundred thousand were not able to get in. It was feared a riot would start when the gates were closed. Everyone seemed to be overcome with grief.

There were dozens of ambulance attendants on duty to care for those who fainted, and they were kept busy. Every couple of minutes, another person would crumple to the floor.

Rick and I were amazed by the outpouring of emotion.

Sure, *we* felt a great sense of loss—but he was our brother. From what was going on in and around Graceland, you would have thought that some mighty king or religious leader had died.

Bags of mail were stacked up six to eight feet deep behind the house, and Graceland's fourteen acres were covered with flowers sent from all over the world.

At one point, Rick looked at me and asked, "Do you think the people were this upset the day Jesus died?"

Rick and I weren't churchgoers—in fact we were far from it. But at the same time, we both knew idolatry when we saw it, and we were disturbed by the general reaction to Elvis's death.

In the days immediately following Elvis's death, Rick spent a lot of time on the phone talking to Robyn. Her talk about Jesus was starting to get through to him, but I knew he was distraught and looking for something—anything—to help him get through his grief. He wasn't ready to become a born-again Christian or anything like that, but I could tell he was thinking seriously about what Robyn was saying. As for me, I wanted nothing to do with it.

At the funeral, he tried to talk to me about his latest conversation with Robyn.

"Rick," I said impatiently, "I don't give a damn about any of that!"

Elvis's funeral was really strange. For some reason, none of us could take it seriously. Elvis himself had always had trouble dealing with funerals, and he had joked his way through them, probably as a defense against showing his grief. We all had the feeling that Elvis was laughing his way through his own funeral, too.

Priscilla was there; so were Linda Thompson, Ginger Alden, Ann-Margret, and many other of Elvis's former girl friends.

Lamar Fike took note of that. "Hey, man! Elvis Presley is the only guy I know who would deliberately die just so he could get all of his girl friends into the same room."

That line got a big laugh, even from Dad.

When Linda and I had a chance to be alone I told her, "Linda, if you had been there...."

"You don't even have to say it, David, I know. He'd still be alive."

Linda had always been so good at looking after Elvis. When he got up from bed and went into the bathroom, the cardinal rule, whether you were an employee or a girl friend, was that you stayed awake until he came back to bed. If he wasn't back in twenty minutes or so, you went in and got him.

On the night he died, Ginger was in the room with him. But she didn't get up to check on him. Instead, she fell back to sleep and didn't realize that he hadn't come back to bed until she awoke, late the following morning.

No one can really be sure exactly what happened in those last few hours. My own personal belief is that what happened happened because it was Elvis's time to die.

I've been asked if I've ever given thought to the idea that Elvis ended his life on purpose. My answer is that I just can't believe that, even though he talked so much about his death during the last couple months of his life. Elvis always considered suicide to be the coward's way out. He had turned down the role in *A Star Is Born* because the character killed himself. When television star Freddie Prinze took his own life, Elvis expressed outrage and grief.

Beyond all that, those of us who worked for Elvis had saved his life several times before. Nothing different happened this time, except that we came to his aid too late. I believe that Elvis simply knew the end was approaching and there was nothing he or anyone else could do to change that.

After the service at Graceland, it was time for the trip to the cemetery, where the body would be interred. The procession was sixteen coaches long—sixteen gleaming white Cadillac limousines.

When Ginger came out of the house to get into the hearse,

a huge tree limb fell from one of the trees in the yard and came crashing down, just missing her.

"Look at that," someone joked. "I knew Elvis didn't really care for her!"

"Nah, he's just mad at her because she was asleep when he needed her."

It sounds malicious, but it really wasn't. It was a bizarre type of humor to help get us through this terrible time. And I think that some of us honestly believed Elvis had something to do with that tree limb falling. It wasn't a dead limb; the tree was very much alive. Maybe it was some sort of sign.

It took us more than an hour to reach the cemetery, which was only a few miles from Graceland. On every corner stood a policeman in full-dress uniform, all of them saluting us.

Thousands upon thousands of people lined the road all the way to the cemetery. Photographers and film crews were everywhere, including above us. Helicopters filled the sky, as cameramen covered the procession from every conceivable angle.

Finally we arrived at the cemetery, Elvis's body was sealed into the mausoleum, and it was all over.

It's hard for me to put into words how I felt. It seemed that all the world was mourning Elvis's death. Everyone seemed to feel his loss, but my pain was incredible. People who didn't even know him except through his records and movies felt like they had lost a personal friend, but I had lost my brother and one of the closest friends I could ever have. And Elvis had been much more to me than a brother; he had been a brother, a father, a teacher, a friend. Whenever I needed someone, I knew I could count on Elvis—and now I would never see him again.

Leaving the cemetery that August afternoon, I felt like I was leaving the best part of me behind. My head hurt. My eyes stung. I wanted to cry—I needed to cry—but the tears wouldn't come. I felt as if I were going to explode from all the grief trapped inside me.

The next few days, I spent all of my time drinking or smoking dope. What else was there to do? I had nothing to look forward to, no reason to get out of bed in the morning. My wife was gone, Elvis was gone, and life didn't hold anything else for me. Reality was painful, something to be avoided.

After a few days, I figured I ought to go back up to Graceland and talk to Dad. Vernon had always been a big, robust man, but he was looking frail, weak, and especially old. Elvis's death had taken its toll.

We sat in the dining room, at the table where we had spent so many happy times together as a family, and talked.

"What do you think, David?" he asked me. "Do you want to stay on?"

"I don't know. . . ." I really hadn't thought about the future at all.

I decided finally to leave, and I went by the office to pick up my final paycheck. I realized as I did so that I was totally on my own.

More than once Elvis had said to me, "You'll never have to worry about a thing, because I'll always look after you," but now he was gone.

I've been asked if I expected Elvis to leave me a lot of money. No, I didn't. When he told me he would take care of me, I knew he wasn't talking about money. I wasn't surprised when he left everything he had to his daughter. Lisa Marie was always the brightest joy of Elvis's life.

Immediately after the funeral, Rick left Tennessee for Los Angeles. He wanted me to come with him. We knew the entertainment business. We had some contacts. Maybe something would happen for us out there.

But I said no. Instead, I headed for Nashville, where I moved into an apartment with a friend of mine. You can guess what was on my mind. Maybe I could talk Angie into coming back to me.

I spent several weeks trying, but Elvis had been right when he told me the marriage was over.

Meanwhile, Rick kept calling. "Come on out to L.A., David. We could both use a fresh start."

Finally, I decided he was right.

I called him and said, "I'll be out there tomorrow."

"You will?" He chuckled. "That's great, except I'm leaving today . . . for Florida." He was on his way to see Robyn. The girl was really getting through to him!

My stay in Los Angeles didn't last very long—two weeks to be exact. That was how long it took me to find out that whatever I was looking for wasn't there. And I was still getting those long-distance phone calls from Rick, only now it was, "David, come on down to Florida!"

Well, why not? Somewhere there had to be a remedy for this ache and loneliness I felt. Maybe I'd find the answer in Florida.

So October of 1977 found me blinking back the Florida sunshine, trying to figure out if this was really Rick standing before me. He looked like Rick, and he sounded like Rick, but he sure didn't act like Rick. Rick had been an emaciated, wild-eyed druggie—a man who would shoot anything into his veins if he could melt it down. Now here he was, stone-cold sober, telling me he had no need for drugs or alcohol. He didn't even want to smoke pot with me.

"What in the world happened to you, Rick?"

"I met Jesus Christ!"

"Oh, come on!" That was about the last thing I expected to hear from Reckless Rick.

When Rick had arrived in Florida, strung out as usual, Robyn's family had offered to put him in a drug treatment center at their expense. But a funny thing happened on his way to the center. Rick had attended a church service in a storefront church. During the service, Rick told me, he had been "saved" and "instantly delivered" from his addiction.

Saved I understood. *Delivered* I didn't.

"I don't know what you're talking about," I told him.

"David, my desire for drugs just left me. It's gone . . . just like that!"

All the time I was in Florida, Rick preached at me. Jesus loved me and could change my life. Jesus could heal all my hurt, and on and on. I had always believed in Jesus as the Son of God, but this kind of talk was more than I could take. Good old Rick had been transformed into a goody-goody, and I almost felt like I was losing another brother.

I told him how I felt.

"Rick, just forget all this Jesus stuff. I don't care!"

I didn't like the fact that he was always telling me I didn't need drugs or booze. Who was he to be telling me what to do? I was the one who had saved his life when he overdosed, and now he was preaching to me. My drugs were about all I had left.

Finally, I had had enough, so I headed back to Memphis. Mom was there, and I could move in with her. But going from Rick to Mom wasn't much of an improvement. She was always praying for me, and I couldn't make up my mind which was worse: being preached at or prayed at.

One night I stayed at her house while she went out on a date. I had a bottle of Valiums and a fifth of whiskey. I took two Valiums, and nothing seemed to happen, so I took two more ... and then two more. Pretty soon I was gulping handfuls of them, washing them down with the whiskey.

Then everything went black.

I woke up in the hospital three days later, with a doctor peering down at me.

"You're supposed to be dead," he said.

I had IVs in both my arms and tubes running up my nose.

Behind the doctor, I could see someone else. My vision was blurry; I couldn't seem to get my eyes to focus. But I knew it was my mother, and I knew she was praying. "Please, Lord," I heard her say, "let my boy be all right!"

I found out later the only reason I survived was that my mother had forgotten something. She asked her date to stop by the house for a minute so she could pick it up. When she came in, she found me unconscious on the floor. They rushed me to the hospital, where my stomach was pumped and my life was saved. Had Mom not come by the house for another hour or two, I would have died.

After I got out of the hospital, I asked Shelley and Arilla if I could move in with them. They said fine, so that's what I did. I was grateful to Mom for saving my life, but I still wasn't ready for all that religious stuff of hers. Being around it made me nervous! So for most of the next two years Shelley and Arilla fed me, clothed me, and generally took care of me, while I sat around and drank and took drugs.

For several months I didn't work, I didn't look for work, and I didn't care.

Did anything happen in 1978? If it did, I missed it, because I was zonked out on one thing or another. There were several overdoses—some mild and others not so mild. But through it all Shelley and Arilla put up with me and tried to help me.

I didn't see Dad very much during that time. We talked once in a while, but he was not doing well. He had a very bad heart, and it was obvious that he wasn't going to be around a whole lot longer.

For a while, I left Memphis and went back to California. Priscilla helped get me into commercial acting school, and I was in a couple of commercials. It looked like I was starting to put the pieces back together. Then I just decided it wasn't what I wanted to do. I had offers from several rock bands, which wanted me to go to work either in security or as a road manager, but I just didn't think I could handle it.

Finally, without giving anyone any notice, I headed back for Memphis, where I showed up on Shelley and Arilla's doorstep. Once more, they took me in without hesitation.

And once more, the days began to flash by in a drug-induced blur.

I was dating a girl named Tommie at this time, and one night we were walking along Cooper Street, near Overton Square, and we started arguing about something. I don't remember what we were fighting about, except that I was terribly depressed, as usual, and had been taking Valiums and Quaaludes as well as drinking beer.

Another girl, a friend of Tommie's, saw us arguing and decided she was going to get into the act.

She charged up to me. "You lousy jerk! You probably killed Elvis!" Every other word was a swear word, and she was really letting me have it.

I knew people were looking at us, and I was embarrassed; so I turned my back on her and started to walk away. But she wasn't finished with me. Instead, she ran around in front of me and slapped me hard, on my cheek.

That was enough. Without thinking, I reached out with my right and sent her flying. I left her lying on the sidewalk, minus two of her teeth, and then turned and walked across the street.

As soon as I got to the other side, a police car pulled up alongside me, lights flashing. A policeman jumped out, threw me up against the side of the car, and began frisking me. Then he put me in the backseat and took me to jail. I stayed there overnight, until Arilla came and had me released the next morning.

During my time in jail I kept thinking about how far I had fallen. I had been riding around the country on a private jet, eating in the best restaurants, practically throwing money away. And now, here I was a drunken druggie, of no use to anyone. What could I do with my life? I didn't even have a high school education. I was drowning in an ocean of self-pity.

Finally, I decided I'd have to get a job. I wound up pumping gas at the same airport where we used to keep the *Lisa Marie*. I would watch the planes come and go—from the small prop jobs to the sleek, flashy jets—and all I could think about was the old days. I wanted to be able to tell people about those days and what it had been like jetting around the country with Elvis Presley. But I knew no one could comprehend the life I had shared with Elvis, and that added to my frustration.

Every day passed in exactly the same way. In the morning I got up and went to work. In the evening, as soon as I got home, I started in with the drinking and the drugs. When I had a day off, that only meant I started in with the drugs and drinking a little earlier than usual.

Then I lost even my minimum-wage job pumping gas and wound up working as a bouncer in a strip joint. By that time I was at the point where I hated myself. I was a drugged-out drunk with no money whatsoever.

After my stint as a bouncer, I went to work for an Elvis Presley impersonator. That was really strange. All those years I had spent traveling around the country with the real Elvis, and now here I was, a flunky for a man who was at best a pale imitation of the real thing. It was almost eerie watching him pretend to be my dead brother.

Six weeks of that was all I could take, and then I was back out on the streets. I had no goals, no direction for my life, and I wouldn't listen to anyone who tried to talk to me.

From time to time, I would talk to Rick. He seemed so happy. He and Robyn were married and he was even preaching occasionally. Some of the things he told me were totally foreign—almost beyond my comprehension. Every time I talked to him, I'd hang up the phone thinking, *Is this the same guy I used to know?*

I'd talk to my mother once in a while, too, but not very often. Between Rick and my mother I was getting all the religion I could handle.

Some of my other friends seemed to have given up on me. Jimmy Marberry had talked to me several times, and told me I was killing myself with the drugs and the booze. He had pleaded with me, threatened me, and tried in every other way he knew to get me to change my ways, but it did no good. Finally, he told me that if I wanted to kill myself in this way, he couldn't stop me. But he wasn't going to sit around and watch it happen. And from that day on, he left me pretty much alone.

I didn't have a great deal of contact with my stepfather. He was in increasingly poor health. He was in and out of the intensive care unit of Baptist Hospital, because of his heart condition. He had gone rapidly downhill since Elvis died— and I didn't like to be around him because it was painful to see how bad he looked. It wasn't that I didn't love him and care about him. It's really that I cared too much. I was at such a low point in my own life that I simply could not face up to his illness.

During the spring of 1979, Dad went into the hospital for the last time. There were so many things I wanted to say to him, but I knew if I tried to say them my mouth would go dry and the words wouldn't come out. So I sat down and wrote him a letter.

I told him that he had been a good father, that I loved him, and appreciated his taking us into his family. I tried my best to let him know how grateful I was for all of the things he had done for my brothers and me over the years.

Later on, the nurse who had been with him told me that he had cried when he read the letter. He told her that he had always been proud of his sons and that he loved us very much.

I will always wish I could have said those words to him in person, but I was so far down in the gutter that I couldn't. On June 26, 1979, Vernon Presley died.

Once again, the family would be brought together in a time of sorrow. As we gathered at Graceland for the funeral, a clean-cut young man came walking into the room with a Bible in his hand. This must be the evangelist who was going to conduct the service. Wait a minute? This was—no, it couldn't be—but it was! This was Rick Stanley!

He was totally transformed. He had put on about fifty pounds, which means he was at his perfect weight, his hair was neatly trimmed, and he was wearing a good-looking suit. When I had seen Rick in Florida, a year and a half earlier, I had been surprised that he was off drugs. But I figured that his "religious" phase would pass. Now, seeing him again, it was obvious that something real had happened to him. His whole life had been changed. His face was glowing with health—and what was even more startling was the calmness that seemed to surround him.

It's not right to say he seemed happy, because he was saddened by Dad's passing. But at the same time, he seemed to be serene and peaceful. I don't really know how to describe how I felt. My life was aimless, hopeless, without purpose. On the other hand, Rick seemed to have it all together—he seemed to know what life was all about.

My first words to him were, "Rick! You look weird!"

He laughed. "Have you looked in a mirror lately?"

Well, perhaps *weird* wasn't exactly the word I had been looking for.

"What in the world happened to you?" I tried again.

"You know what happened to me," he said. "I was saved!"

"Are you trying to tell me that. . . ."

"David, I wish more than anything else that you could have what I have. I could stand here and talk about it all day, but until you experience it yourself, you're not going to understand what I'm talking about."

I stood there and shook my head.

After the funeral, I asked Rick if we could get away somewhere, just the two of us, and talk. I was fascinated by the change in Rick and wanted to find out more about what had caused it.

If I took a photo of the way Rick looked on the day Elvis died, and another photo of the way he looked at Vernon's funeral, and put them in a magazine as a before-and-after advertisement, I have no doubt that millions of people would write in to buy whatever brought about such a change for the better.

Rick and I went to a coffee shop, and I sat and listened, while he told me all about his new life-style. He didn't take drugs, he didn't drink, and he didn't smoke. He was happily married to Robyn, and he didn't run around on his wife.

"I only have one question," I told him. "Just what *do* you do?"

He leaned back in the booth and laughed. "You know what I do! I praise the Lord!"

It all sounded so corny to me. But I couldn't doubt my eyes. It was most definitely for real.

"Look, David, why don't you come down to Florida and stay with Robyn and me for a while?"

I drained the last bit of coffee from my cup. "Nah, I don't think—"

"Why not? What's holding you here?"

"Nothing," I had to admit.

"So, you don't have to stay. Just come on down and see what our life is like. If nothing else, it'll give us a chance to catch up on all the latest."

"What would Robyn say?"

"She'd love it! She'd be glad to have you."

"You sure?"

"Positive!"

He had talked me into it.

By this time, Rick was working with an evangelist named Moody Adams, and he was traveling around, preaching in different churches. Rick's story of how God had picked him up and changed his life was an impressive one, and he usually received an enthusiastic response. The first time I saw him preach and quote from the Bible, my mind drifted back to the time Elvis and I had to go get him out of jail. He had looked so pathetic.

Rick and Robyn had a profound effect on me. When I looked at them I knew, more than ever, that my life wasn't what it ought to be. Rick often preached about the Holy Spirit convicting people who were living in sin, and I knew firsthand what he was talking about.

My conscience troubled me a great deal, because I knew my life was a mess. But still I resisted. I told myself that I wasn't really "messed up." I was just wild, a rebel. And I enjoyed being that way. I certainly didn't want to do anything that would cramp my style.

Still, I stayed on in Florida.

* * *

Early in 1980, Rick asked me to accompany him on an evangelistic trip to Canada. We spent several weeks in that country, and every night I listened as Rick preached his heart out.

One night during the service, I slipped outside, into the cold Canadian air, and had a short talk with God.

I looked up at the sky. There must have been a million stars, and the moon was full and bright.

"I don't understand," I whispered. "I'd like to believe everything Rick is saying about You loving us so much ... but I don't understand.

"How could You let Elvis die like he did? And what about my dad? What about all the pain he went through after Elvis died?"

I stood there for perhaps five minutes, waiting for some sort of reply, but none came. All I heard was the rumbling noise of a truck passing by on a nearby street and the drone of a small airplane that passed by to the west. Feeling drained and defeated, I slipped back inside for the rest of the service.

Back in Florida, Rick had big news. He had met an evangelist named James Robison who was the head of a large Christian organization based in Dallas. Robison had been impressed with Rick's preaching and had invited him to come to Dallas and become a part of the team.

"And David, he's looking for a good sound man. I've recommended you to him. I know you'd do a great job."

"But Rick, " I protested, "I'm not ready to do that. I'm no preacher."

"You don't have to be a preacher. Just a good sound man."

"Nah . . . it's just not for me."

So once again, we went our separate ways. Rick and Robyn left for Texas, and I went back to Memphis, where I resumed my old life-style.

One night as I was looking through the newspaper, trying to find something to watch on TV, my eye fell across a small ad at the bottom of the page.

Tonight, at eight o'clock, evangelist James Robison would be preaching on the subject of. . . .

I looked at my watch. It was eight-fifteen. Well, I might as well turn it on, and find out what this Robison guy was all about.

I'll never forget that evening, because I was drinking a beer, smoking a joint, and watching a Christian evangelist on TV. And he was preaching a sermon based on John 3:16: "For God so loved the world, that he gave his only begotten Son. . . ."

As I thought about that particular verse from the Bible, I began to understand for the first time what it was really saying. I thought back to the time when Elvis had read the verse during a concert, and I remembered how moved I had been then.

I thought about my one-way conversation with God that night in Canada. Had this been God's answer all along? I thought about how much it hurt me to see Elvis die and to lose my father. And that made me think, for the first time in my life, about how much it must have hurt God to watch His Son die. I thought about Mom and all those Sundays and Wednesday nights I'd spent in church because of her. I thought about all those lessons I had learned in Vacation Bible School—things I had tried so hard to leave behind. I began thinking about Robyn and how she had gone to such great lengths to tell Rick about Jesus' love.

Finally, I started thinking about Jesus Christ Himself. I thought about how two thousand years ago, He was standing in a garden when His enemies came and arrested Him, without reason. I thought about how they took Him before Pontius Pilate and unjustly accused Him of committing crimes against the state. There, they stripped off His robe and pushed onto His head a crown made out of thorns. They beat Him, kicked Him, spit on Him, and sarcastically bowed down before Him, treating the Son of God as if He were worthy only of their contempt and cruelty. Then they threw a cross on His back and marched Him up a hill called Calvary, where He was nailed to the cross and lifted up to die. But He wasn't dying for things He had done. He was dying for you and me, tasting the pain and anguish we deserve, so that we can stand blameless before God.

There on that hill, with His arms outstretched and His lifeblood draining away, Jesus Christ called out, "Father, forgive them; for they know not what they do ..." (Luke 23:34). And now I realized that Jesus was calling for forgiveness not only for those who were putting Him to death that day. He was saying, "Father, forgive the murderers! Forgive the thieves! Forgive the adulterers! Forgive the druggies! Forgive Dave Stanley!" He was seeking forgiveness for you, no matter who you are or what you may have done.

And, after He had said that, He bowed his head and died—temporarily.

They took His body down and put it in a tomb. But three days later, Jesus did something nobody else could ever do. John F. Kennedy didn't do it. Neither did John Lennon or Jimi Hendrix. Elvis Presley couldn't do it. What Jesus Christ did was, He rose from the dead and walked out of that tomb. He had overcome mankind's greatest enemy: death! And all who believe in Him have overcome death through Him!

As I thought about all of that, I realized my life was way out of line. I had been on a fast track to hell, and only Jesus could turn me around.

That Sunday found me in church, listening to a preacher named Freddie Gage, as he preached another sermon—simple and yet powerful—straight out of the Bible. I liked what he had to say and was impressed by the fact that he didn't pull any punches. He told it like it was, with no holding back. I had always been a direct, upfront person myself. I had little patience with people who couldn't come straight to the point, or who waited to see how everyone else felt before telling you what they thought.

Freddie Gage was most definitely not that way. He painted a clear black-and-white picture of sin and righteousness, of hope and hopelessness, of heaven and hell.

After the service, I hung around so I could get a chance to talk with him. I told him how much I enjoyed his sermon, told him who I was, and mentioned that my brother Rick had just gone to work for the Robison organization.

"Oh, I know Rick," he said. "He's a fine young man."

"Yeah, he is," I agreed. "He was after me to apply for a job as a sound man, but...."

"You ought to do it," he said. "They're still looking for someone, and I know you're qualified."

I nodded. "I just might do that."

I stuck out my hand, and he grasped it firmly.

"But, David," he said, "you might want to get a haircut and uh, dress up a little bit before you go interview for the job."

Immediately, I could feel the anger. The old rebellion was rising up—a flash from the past. But I had nowhere else to look but up. Besides, I was looking pretty wild and woolly at the time.

That afternoon I called Rick again. I told him I had made up my mind to apply for that job. Not only that, but I was going to change my life-style. I was going to quit drinking and smoking dope, I was going to get cleaned up and do everything I could do to get myself straight.

"Rick," I told him, "I want to be like you."

That night, I went up to Belleview Baptist Church, where Adrian Rogers is pastor. When the sermon had ended and it was time for the altar call, I went down to the front of the church and told the pastor I wanted to join the church. Over the next few days, I didn't smoke a single joint, or even touch a glass of beer. I got my hair cut and washed my one-and-only pair of jeans.

Within the week, I was in Dallas, interviewing for the position of director of sound communications. To my surprise, I got the job. I was excited and happy. This was the beginning of a whole new life for me.

What I didn't understand was that there was still one major difference between Rick and me. Namely, I had determined through my own strength that I was going to be a better person. I was going to join a church and act right. I was going to do it all by myself, without God's help. Rick was operating in the power of God. I had determined that I was going to be a good person; Rick had experienced an encounter with God that left him no real choice in the matter!

Back home in Memphis, I gathered all my things and prepared for the trip to Dallas.

Once again, Arilla and Shelley bid me good-bye. I'm sure they were thinking that I'd be back. They had seen me come and go so many times before.

I didn't have much to take with me. Some photographs of Elvis and me, a few changes of underwear, a toothbrush . . . and that was about it. I had one pair of jeans and a T-shirt and only one dime in my pocket.

I had had just enough money to fill my 1970 Mustang with gasoline—and I hoped that would get me the 450 miles to Dallas. Somehow I knew I wasn't coming back. This time, I was sure that things were about to roll my way!

Twelve

Yes, Lord

"Give me a break, D. J.," I said. "There's about as much chance of that as there is of a blizzard on the Fourth of July."

"I'm telling you, David, the girl likes you." He flashed me a mischievous grin. "You're going to wind up marrying that girl."

D. J. was one of my closest friends at James Robison headquarters. He was teasing me about a girl named Kandis, a pretty young secretary who had started working there about the same time I had. Kandis had just graduated from Baylor University with a degree in education. She was working as a secretary until a teaching position opened up.

"Don't tell me you haven't had your eye on her!" he teased me.

I laughed. "Okay, you caught me. But that doesn't mean she'd have anything to do with me."

Kandis Lanier was a very special lady. In my mind, she was like a porcelain angel. I didn't know girls like her really existed. I had been attracted to her the first time I saw her.

She was a petite, green-eyed beauty, with a smile that could make my heart beat faster.

But the thing that impressed me most about Kandis was that she seemed so gentle, so loving, so . . . pure. I figured she was just about perfect, and whenever I was close to her, my own past seemed that much worse. I knew she would never want to have anything to do with me, especially once she found out what my life had been like before I joined the James Robison team.

I was living around Christians, so I was doing my best to fit in. I was talking their language, and I was trying to live the life, but down in my heart, I felt that I really wasn't as good as they were.

Then another friend of mine, a guy named Terry, started telling me about Kandis, too.

"You ought to ask her out. She's really nice, and I think you two would get along great."

"But I don't even know her," I protested.

"Whose fault is that?"

Okay, I would at least try to get to know her. I'd stop and talk to her, but I was still too much in awe of her to ask her out on a date.

I was doing okay in Dallas, but sometimes I felt terribly alone. Rick was out on the road preaching just about all of the time, and most of my friends were still in Memphis.

One night, when I was feeling terribly depressed and alone, I got down on my knees and started praying: "God, I'm so lonely. I'm so tired of not having anyone. Would You please send me someone to care about."

Almost as soon as I finished praying, the telephone rang. It was Kandis.

"Hi, David. I was just wondering if . . . well, there's a Baylor football game Saturday. I was wondering if you'd like to go with me."

"Sure!"

We had a good time together at the football game, but I was disappointed to find out that there was another man in her life, someone she had dated regularly for some time. When she told me that her relationship with the other guy didn't seem to be going anywhere, I had to fight back a smile. One point for my side.

I was hopeful, because I knew she wouldn't have asked me to go to the game with her if she didn't like me. But then, maybe she only asked me because she wanted to provoke him to jealousy. I was playing all sorts of psychological games with myself, trying to figure out what her motives were.

Two weeks later, Baylor had its homecoming game. I wanted to ask Kandis to go with me, but before I had a chance, she told me she was going with the other guy—my rival.

I was jubilant the next day when she called and told me she and her friend had had a terrible time at the game. They had fought most of the time, and just didn't seem to enjoy being together. Then she asked me if I'd like to come over and watch some TV with her. Would I ever!

For the next six weeks, we were together almost every day. I was either at her house watching TV, we were out on a date, or we were in church. We spent a lot of time in church. What a contrast from most of the girls I had known while I was working for Elvis!

For that entire six weeks, I didn't kiss her. I didn't even try. The more I got to know her, the more impressed I was. She had grown up in a Christian family, she sang in the choir, she taught Sunday school. In my mind, she was the personification of sweetness and light.

One night I finally got up my courage and decided that I was going to kiss her. Just a little kiss. It wasn't really so much that I decided I was going to kiss her as it was that I *had* to, because my feelings for her were so strong. But once I kissed her, it was all over. It was, "Let's go ahead and order the wedding cake" time.

We set the wedding date for six months away, March 6, 1981.

I was ecstatic, but not everyone around Kandis felt that

way. Some of her friends knew about my sordid past, and they were aghast that she should even think of marrying me. They told her I was an ex-junkie and an ex-hell-raiser and that she should just stay away from me.

But Kandis knew I loved her, and she also knew that I had been entirely honorable toward her during the six weeks we had been dating. Luckily for me, she wasn't going to let anyone talk her out of marrying me.

During the months leading up to our wedding, I also began to rethink what I wanted to do with my life. I enjoyed working for James Robison. But then I started remembering what it had been like back in 1966, when I was baptized at Westhaven Church of Christ in Memphis. I had felt at that time that God wanted me to be a preacher someday, and those dusty old feelings were coming back stronger than ever.

During this time, I began doing quite a bit of traveling with John McKay, Jr., who was the director of music for the James Robison Evangelistic Association. John was an excellent singer, who was often called to give concerts. When he went out on the road, I went with him, so I could handle the audio equipment. It was John who first asked me to stand up and share in front of an audience what Jesus had done in my life. From the very first, people responded enthusiastically to me, and John began asking me to speak more often. He supported me and encouraged me in my desire to be out preaching the gospel.

I was always amazed at how comfortable I felt in the pulpit. It was easy for me to stand up in front of people and tell them how God had brought me through all the hard times. I knew that being Elvis Presley's stepbrother was opening doors for me, but at the same time, my message was always that God was using me not because I was Elvis's brother, but rather in spite of the fact that I was Elvis's brother. Like the Apostle Paul, I often thought of myself as the "chiefest of sinners."

I realized that if God could use me, He could use anyone. And He was using me. Whenever I preached, I received an enthusiastic response. But what made the greatest impression on me were the letters and phone calls I received from people telling me how much my story had meant to them. There was a letter from a teenager, telling me that after hearing me he had decided to lay off pot and pills; another from a mother writing to tell me how the Lord had used me to change her daughter's life; and one from an Elvis Presley fan who had come to hear me talk about Elvis, but wound up giving her life to Christ.

I was receiving more and more invitations to speak, so early in 1981 I made a decision to leave the James Robison organization and launch out on my own.

Kandis and I were married on March 6. That same week I resigned as director of sound communications for James Robison and began Dave Stanley Ministries.

Perhaps it would have been better to wait a while, to get on our feet financially before launching out with a new venture. But I simply could not wait. I felt a "fire in my bones" to spend as much of my time as possible traveling around and telling others about the gift of eternal life and the transforming power of Jesus Christ.

The funny thing about that was that I was telling others how they could turn to Christ, but I hadn't really done it myself. I was still operating very much under my own power. I was walking the walk, and talking the talk, but, to put it simply, I was professing but not possessing Jesus. I was doing as I've seen many others do. There was no peace, no joy, no assurance in my life. I believed in what I was doing, and yet so much of it was for my own glory. I didn't even realize it at the time, but looking back now I can see that I wanted people to say, "Boy, that Dave Stanley is a good preacher," every bit as much as I wanted them to say, "Did you hear what Dave Stanley said about Jesus Christ?" As far as my life went, I was leaning on my own good works and on the things I had learned at the Whitehaven Church of Christ, rather than on the saving grace of God.

The words of Ephesians 2:8, 9 had never sunk in: "For by

grace you have been saved through faith, and that not of yourselves; it is the gift of God, not of works, lest anyone should boast"(NKJV).

Then in March of 1982, an amazing thing happened to Kandis. I was preaching in Nashville and when I called home late one Sunday night, Kandis was bubbling over with excitement.

"David," she said breathlessly, "something wonderful happened to me tonight!"

"Oh?"

"I was saved!"

"Saved!" I was astonished. What in the world did she mean by that? Kandis had practically been born in a church building. She had been in church all her life. Surely that meant she was "saved."

"No, David," she explained. "I realized tonight that I had never surrendered my life to Jesus Christ. I was trying to be saved by being good, by attending church, by teaching Sunday school. And you can't be saved by those things."

She paused only for a moment and then kept going. "It's like it says right here, '. . . Whosoever believeth in him. . . .' "

There was that verse again, John 3:16. Kandis went on to tell me that she had come to understand, only tonight, that her eternal destiny did not depend on anything she did, except her belief and trust in Jesus. She had resolved to quit leaning on her own efforts and simply trust God.

"I guess I've heard that for years," she said. "But tonight it was like a light went on!"

Her words hit me hard. I had an empty feeling in the pit of my stomach as I realized that I, too, had been trusting in myself as much as in God. I had quit taking dope, quit drinking, quit smoking, quit running around with loose women. I had been so busy saving myself that I didn't have much time to let God save me!

I remembered a conversation with Priscilla when I told her I was in Dallas and was a part of the Robison organization.

"David," she had warned me, "watch out for those guys." She was suspicious of anyone who preached on TV. Her attitude was that they were probably after money.

"Don't worry about me," I had told her. "It's just a job."

As I thought back on that conversation I wondered if that was the way it still was for me. Was I just doing a job? I didn't want it to be that way.

I realized that I was doing everything right, with one exception. I had never accepted Jesus Christ as my Lord and Savior.

*   *   *

On Tuesday night, March 25, 1982, I was back home in Texas, where I watched Kandis being baptized at First Baptist Church of Euless, where James T. Draper is the pastor. Bailey Smith was preaching that night, and as I listened to him, I knew more than ever that I, too, needed to be saved. But I was so confused. What would all the people think when they saw me walking down the aisle, admitting that I had never really surrendered my life to Christ? They knew I had been out on the road, telling thousands of people how Jesus could change their lives. Wouldn't they be surprised and disappointed by my admission that I myself was not saved?

I was in turmoil! I wanted to walk down the aisle, and yet I just couldn't. I had to. But I couldn't make my way out of my pew! Thank God for a long-winded music director. Finally, I broke the bonds that were holding me back. "Devil," I said, "you go to hell where you belong," and I walked down to the front of the church. That night I was saved, and I walked out of the church a new creature in Jesus Christ.

From that day on, my ministry changed drastically. The invitations began to pour in, I began to receive promptings about which sermons to preach on which nights, and the response was much greater than ever before. It hit me one night, too, that I was no longer interested in attracting attention to myself. I wanted to attract their attention to Jesus. Always before I had thought, *I want to be like Rick, or Freddie Gage, or my pastor Jimmy Draper.* But now, I knew beyond any doubt that I really wanted to be like Jesus Christ.

Not that I became perfect or that I became totally selfless, a man without an ego. My years with Elvis spoiled me in a lot of ways, and I see that selfishness coming to the surface every now and then. But before and after being saved, the difference has been tremendous.

March of 1982 was a very big month for Kandis and me in other ways, too. We bought our first house, and shortly after that, we found out that Kandis was pregnant. We were overjoyed and yet a bit frightened, too. Kandis is a diabetic, and the doctor told us that the pregnancy would not be easy. She would have to go to the doctor three times a week and take blood tests twice a day.

The doctor told her that he wanted to hear from her at the first sign of anything abnormal. I remember how she came home from the doctor in tears after he told her she could have a miscarriage at any time.

I was away from home most of the time during the nine months of her pregnancy and was preaching out of town every weekend. Even when I was at home, I wasn't able to give her as much attention as she probably needed. In 1981 I had taken the test and received my G.E.D., the equivalent of a high school diploma. And then I had enrolled in Tarrant County Junior College, where I was taking an eighteen-hour course load.

But everywhere I preached, I asked the people to pray for Kandis and the baby—and she sailed through the pregnancy.

On December 22, 1982, Austin Aaron Stanley was born, capping off a marvelous year. The hospital put the baby in a stocking with his little blanket, and the words *Merry Christmas* were written across the stocking. I thought when

I saw him how appropriate that was. He was our special Christmas present from a loving Father.

Throughout 1983 and into 1984, my ministry continued to grow. Invitations were coming from everywhere—so many that I couldn't possibly accept them all. And after I had spoken, the letters would come, telling me how God had used me to touch hearts and lives. I often wept as I read them.

I remember one letter in particular, from a man, telling me that his teenage son had been involved in drugs and making a complete mess of his life. He came to church to hear me on a Sunday morning, only because he was interested in Elvis. But after hearing my sermon, he had accepted Jesus as his personal Savior. That afternoon, he had been so excited that he had talked to several of his friends about the Lord, even getting them to agree to come to church and hear me speak that night. Tragically, before evening came, the young man was in an automobile accident and died instantly.

"Thanks to you," his father wrote, "I have no doubt that my son is in heaven with Jesus and that I will see him again someday." How could I not be moved to tears when I read a letter such as that one?

*   *   *

In the summer of 1984 Priscilla was in Dallas, where she was filming some scenes for the TV show "Dallas." I hadn't seen her in about four years, so I made arrangements to go over to her hotel for a visit.

We talked about the old days for a few minutes, and then she asked, "What are you doing now, David?"

"I'm preaching Jesus—sharing with young people all over the world that there is an answer to all of life's problems."

"Just like your brother."

"That's right."

She looked directly into my eyes. "Well, tell me. Is that just your job?"

"No, Priscilla," I assured her. "It's much more than a job. There are a lot of kids out there who are like I was. They're freaked out, on drugs passed around like a pack of cigarettes. They have everything in the world, but they don't have Jesus. And they need Jesus!"

I could see tears glistening in Priscilla's eyes as she said, "What you're doing must be very rewarding."

I had told her how I felt, and I realized that to push harder would only drive a wedge between us. I hoped I had given her something to think seriously about.

*　　*　　*

In February of 1985, I was in Los Angeles, where there was a party thrown by Joe Esposito for many of Elvis's former employees and friends. I hadn't seen Joe, Jerry Schilling, Larry Geller, a lot of those people for several years.

And everybody kept talking about how different Rick and I looked. I hoped so! The last time they had seen us we were pretty far down the road to nowhere.

Here were people who had known me for twenty years. They watched me grow up into the toughest, meanest head-hunter in all of Elvis's group, and now I was talking to young people and showing them how Jesus Christ could change their lives.

"Man!" Joe said. "You really have changed!"

Pretty soon, Joe got out a stack of photographs. He was a good photographer and had hundreds of photos from the years with Elvis.

"Hey, David, remember this one?" He'd pass around a photo of me smoking a joint, and everyone would have a good laugh. "And this was in Vegas, I think!" Here I'd be clowning around with my arm around some girl I didn't even know, a glazed look on my face.

I laughed right along with everyone else. "Yeah, those are something else. But let me show you something!"

I pulled out a picture of me standing in the pulpit, with an open Bible in my hand. People began passing around the older pictures, comparing them with the one of me preaching. I could feel the presence of God come into the room.

"Yeah," I said, "I loved to smoke dope. And I bet I could have drunk almost any of you under the table back then. Those days were a lot of fun—but they were nothing compared with the fun I have now when I'm standing up in front of hundreds of people, telling them how they can have eternal life."

"David," Jerry Schilling asked, "do you think I could have a copy of this picture?"

Just about everyone else wanted photos, too. I autographed them all, and added my favorite Bible verse, from Psalm 139.

"You know," I told the group at the party, "when Elvis Presley died it was the worst day in my life. No doubt about it.

"But I realize now that if Elvis hadn't died, Rick and I would have. But God had other plans for us. He wanted us to share the gospel.

"I think that for a little while, the world needed someone like Elvis Presley. And I think that his memory should live on. But from now until forever, this world will always need Jesus Christ!"

To God be the glory.

Information pertaining to speaking engagements may be obtained by writing to:

P.O. Box 1025
Euless, Texas 76039

I hope you have enjoyed reading this book on my life with Elvis Presley. It is compiled of only some of the many events that took place in the seventeen years I lived with and worked for my brother. I would appreciate it if you would drop me a letter and let me know your thoughts after reading it. If you enclose a self-addressed stamped envelope in your letter I will send you, free of charge, a full-color, four-by-five-inch photograph of Elvis and myself taken on tour.

I thank you for loving Elvis. . . . And I thank God for allowing Elvis to be a part of my spiritual journey.

> Send letters to: Dave Stanley
> P.O. Box 9100
> Kansas City, Missouri 64168